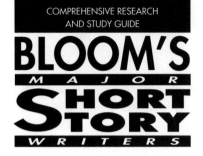

COMPREHENSIVE RESEARCH
AND STUDY GUIDE

BLOOM'S
MAJOR
SHORT
STORY
WRITERS

Herman
Melville

EDITED AND WITH AN
INTRODUCTION BY HAROLD BLOOM

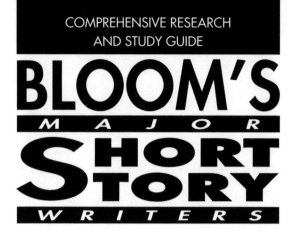

COMPREHENSIVE RESEARCH
AND STUDY GUIDE

BLOOM'S

MAJOR

SHORT STORY

WRITERS

Herman

Melville

EDITED AND   BLOOM

3 5 7 9 8 6 4

Library of Congress Cataloging-in-Publication Data
Herman Melville / edited and with an introduction by Harold Bloom.
p.   cm. – (Bloom's major short story writers)
Includes bibliographical references and index.
ISBN 0-7910-5118-8
Melville, Herman, 1819-1891—Criticism and interpretation—
Handbooks, manuals, etc.   2. Melville, Herman, 1819-1891—
Examinations—Study guides.   3. Short story—Examinations—
Study guides.   4. Short story—Handbooks, manuals, etc.
I. Bloom, Harold.   II. Series.
PS2387.H4   1998
813'.3—dc21
98-31663
CIP

Chelsea House Publishers
1974 Sproul Road, Suite 400
Broomall, PA 19008-0914

www.chelseahouse.com

Contributing Editor: Jennifer Lewin

Contents

User's Guide

This volume is designed to present biographical, critical, and bibliographical information on the author's best-known or most important short stories. Following Harold Bloom's editor's note and introduction is a detailed biography of the author, discussing major life events and important literary accomplishments. A plot summary of each short story follows, tracing significant themes, patterns, and motifs in the work, and an annotated list of characters supplies brief information on the main characters in each story.

A selection of critical extracts, derived from previously published material from leading critics, analyzes aspects of each short story. The extracts consist of statements from the author, if available, early reviews of the work, and later evaluations up to the present. A bibliography of the author's writings (including a complete list of all books written, cowritten, edited, and translated), a list of additional books and articles on the author and the work, and an index of themes and ideas in the author's writings conclude the volume.

~

Harold Bloom is Sterling Professor of the Humanities at Yale University and Henry W. and Albert A. Berg Professor of English at the New York University Graduate School. He is the author of over 20 books and the editor of more than 30 anthologies of literary criticism.

Professor Bloom's works include *Shelley's Mythmaking* (1959), *The Visionary Company* (1961), *Blake's Apocalypse* (1963), *Yeats* (1970), *A Map of Misreading* (1975), *Kabbalah and Criticism* (1975), and *Agon: Toward a Theory of Revisionism* (1982). *The Anxiety of Influence* (1973) sets forth Professor Bloom's provocative theory of the literary relationships between the great writers and their predecessors. His most recent books include *The American Religion* (1992), *The Western Canon* (1994), *Omens of Millennium: The Gnosis of Angels, Dreams, and Resurrection* (1996), and *Shakespeare: The Invention of the Human* (1998).

Professor Bloom earned his Ph.D. from Yale University in 1955 and has served on the Yale faculty since then. He is a 1985 MacArthur Foundation Award recipient and served as the Charles Eliot Norton Professor of Poetry at Harvard University in 1987–88. He is currently the editor of other Chelsea House series in literary criticism, including BLOOM'S NOTES, BLOOM'S MAJOR POETS, MAJOR LITERARY CHARACTERS, MODERN CRITICAL VIEWS, MODERN CRITICAL INTERPRETATIONS, and WOMEN WRITERS OF ENGLISH AND THEIR WORKS.

Editor's Note

My Introduction comments briefly upon all four of the stories or novellas, stressing their Shakespearean overtones. As there are about thirty excerpts giving Critical Views, I confine my editor's remarks here to only a few high points.

Jorge Luis Borges, the Argentine fabulist, finds "Bartleby, the Scrivener" to be a precursor of Kafka's recalcitrant protagonists, while Edgar A. Dryden usefully uncovers the literary allusions and echoes in "The Encantadas."

"Benito Cereno," which remains one of the most difficult of Melville's works, is darkly illuminated by Eric J. Sundquist's observations on the inscrutable nature of the story's protagonists.

Billy Budd, Melville's enigmatic legacy, is classically analyzed by F. O. Matthiessen, who emphasizes our empathy with Captain Vere, after which Barbara Johnson performs her celebrated deconstruction of some elements in the story's language.

Introduction

HAROLD BLOOM

Shakespeare, foremost of writers, deeply affected Melville's art, both in *Moby-Dick* and in the shorter fiction. Captain Ahab broods aloud in the mode of Macbeth, while Claggart is manifestly a version of Iago. Even "Bartleby, the Scrivener," which on its surface owes more to Charles Dickens, is indebted to Shakespeare's mastery of ellipsis, the art of leaving-out. What matters most in Melville's story is never said; an enormous pathos is hinted, but is not expressed. Bartleby and the narrator barely can speak to one another, yet abysses could be explored between them. When the narrator murmurs that the dead Bartleby is asleep "With kings and counsellors," we are startled by the aesthetic dignity of the Jobean but thoroughly Shakespearean evocation, and yet the surprise vanishes upon reflection. Julius Caesar and Brutus, in what should be their one crucial exchange before the scene of the assassination, share a banal moment of asking and telling the time of day. Edmund and King Lear never address one another, and except for one moment in the wings, Antony and Cleopatra are never left alone together. In the painful scene where the newly crowned Henry V rejects Falstaff, the emancipated monarch does not allow the great wit to say anything. This elliptical mode, a far more prevalent Shakespearean technique than is generally realized, prompts Melville's reticences in "Bartleby, the Scrivener."

"The Encantadas" is overtly Spenserian and Bunyanesque, but more darkly it refracts *The Tempest*. In "Sketch Seventh" the Creole Dog-King is a savage parody of Prospero, ruling his Enchanted Isle not with Ariel and a band of sprites, but with fierce dogs. "Sketch Ninth" extends the parody, when the dreadful Oberlus overtly identifies himself with Caliban: "This island's mine by Sycorax my mother." Yet Oberlus is more Timon of Athens than Caliban, and "The Encantadas" serves for Melville the purpose effected for Shakespeare by Timon of Athens, the most rancid of tragedies.

"Benito Cereno," which seems to me the masterpiece of Melville's shorter fiction, is a wonderfully enigmatic story in which Captain Delano and Benito Cereno talk past one another in ways that transcend their difficult situation, in which Delano cannot know that

Cereno and his ship are the captives of a slave rebellion. Even when the rescue has been accomplished, the American and the Spanish captains are in different worlds:

> "But these mild trades that now fan your cheek, do they not come with a human-like healing to you? Warm friends, steadfast friends are trades."
>
> "With their steadfastness they but waft me to my tomb, senor," was the foreboding response.
>
> "You are saved," cried Captain Delano, more and more astonished and pained; "you are saved; what has cast such a shadow upon you?"
>
> "The negro."

Prospero tells us that when he is back in Milan, every third thought shall be his grave, even though the great Magus could not be more triumphant. It is not Caliban who is Prospero's shadow of mortality, but the lost vocation of having been an Hermetic sage. Benito Cereno has more than the shadow of Babo upon him; his own vocation as sea-captain is lost, under the shadow that symbolically he terms "the negro." The inwardness of Cereno's reflection, in contrast to Delano's robust outwardness, is a Shakespearean contrast. Cereno is now lost in the growing inward self, most Shakespearean of inventions.

The Adamic Billy Budd is not a Shakespearean figure, which enhances his helplessness at confronting Iago in Claggart. The "monomania" of Claggart clearly derives from Iago's drive to ruin Othello. "Motiveless malignity," Coleridge's phrase for Iago, is far more applicable to Claggart. It would be difficult to accept Claggart, were it not for our experience of Iago. The effect of Shakespeare's Iago upon Melville's Claggart is more than a matter of influence; "contamination" would be an apter word than "influence." Claggart's "natural depravity" is an uncanny transmission from Iago to Melville's evil genius. ✤

Biography of
Herman Melville

(1819–1891)

Herman Melville was born in 1819. His parents, Allan and Maria (nee Gansevoort) Melville, were children of Revolutionary War heroes. Melville's mother, a somewhat provincial, religious woman, descended from a distinguished Dutch family in Albany. Raised as a Boston gentleman, his father became an enterprising urban merchant; when his business failed in 1830 the family moved from Manhattan to Albany. When Melville was twelve years old his father died, leaving Maria destitute with eight children (the cold, stern Mrs. Glendinning in *Pierre* has long been thought to reflect her). His formal schooling ended at fifteen and in his teenage years Melville held temporary jobs, including those of clerk, bookkeeper, farm worker, and teacher.

In 1839 his publishing career began in two ways: "Fragments from a Writing Desk" appeared pseudonymously in *Democratic Press* and *Lansingburgh Advertiser* in May and a month later Melville went on his first sailing voyage, traveling from New York to Liverpool on the *Saint Lawrence*. *Redburn* (1849) describes this journey, which inspired in him a love of sea travel and provided him with an education upon which he relied for many of his commercially successful narratives. After returning to New York and teaching for a year, he sailed the South Seas on the *Acushnet* and deserted ship with Richard Tobias Greene in 1842; *Moby-Dick* (1851) draws upon this eighteen-month trip. The Marquesas Islands he and Greene visited are represented in *Typee* and *Mardi* (published in 1846 and 1849, respectively). During the next three years he traveled aboard the *Lucy Ann* (he was thrown off as a mutineer and escaped with John B. Troy to Tahiti and Eimeo), the Nantucket whaler *Charles and Henry*, and the frigate *United States*. *Omoo* (1847) tells of his experiences in Tahiti as a laborer on a potato farm, and *White-Jacket* (1850) records his life aboard the man-of-war until being discharged in Boston in 1844. His first five sea tales won him a literary reputation in the United States and abroad, as most of them were published in London and New York in the same years. But *Moby-Dick* and its successor, *Pierre* (1852), were critical failures, and the historical romance *Israel Potter* (1856) was tepidly received.

Moby-Dick has attracted much critical attention in this century, and is required reading in most school curricula. Dedicated to Nathaniel Hawthorne, it is an account of a whaling voyage off Nantucket, staged as an allegorical confrontation between man and destiny. Its famous phrases—"the whiteness of the whale" and "all visible objects are but as pasteboard masks"—are indicative of the two poles around which the narrative revolves: a love of surfaces and their details, and a contrasting search for deeply lodged, inner truths underneath those shining outsides. Both kinds of study emerge in the course of the plot, which is interjected with countless discussions of the whale's anatomy, an encyclopedic history of whaling, and legendary and factual accounts of the great white whale's representation in science and art. *Moby-Dick's* characters, from the monomaniacal Captain Ahab, the former cannibal Queequeg, and Tashtego the Gay Header, the madly sermonizing Father Mapple, and the terrible White Whale, to Ismael, the narrator, are unforgettably vivid and tortured in their own ways. The Yankee Starbuck, cool Stubb, and mechanical Flask are the first, second, and third mates. The *Pequod* nearly circles the earth as the vengeful Ahab indulges in his intense quest for the whale which had taken his leg in a previous encounter. Finally, a three-day war against Moby-Dick ends in bloodshed. The *Pequod*, "like Satan, would not sink till she had dragged a living part of heaven along with her, and helmeted herself with it." Ishmael, its survivor, is brought ashore by the whaler *Rachel*.

Five years after *Moby-Dick*, Melville published *The Piazza Tales*, which included the following stories: "Bartleby, the Scrivener," "Benito Cereno," "The Bell-Tower," "The Paradise of Bachelors and the Tartarus of Maids," and "The Encantadas." *Putnam's* magazine had published fourteen of his tales, including those anthologized, between 1853–56. The stories were well-received, especially "The Encantadas" and "Benito Cereno," which were hailed as favorably reminiscent of Melville's sea tales of the late 1840s. After *The Confidence Man*, which appeared in 1857, he wrote no further prose except the novella *Billy Budd*, left incomplete at his death and not discovered and published until 1924.

As Melville's career as a novelist waned, and his financial situation went from unstable to dire, his ambitions as a poet came to fruition. *Battle-Pieces and Aspects of the War* (1866) includes poems that have earned his current reputation as a concise, epigrammatic, and masterful stylist. The forceful, terse poem "The Portent," inspired by John Brown's actions at Harper's Ferry, serves as an epigraph to the collection. Poems like "In the Turret," "At the Cannon's Mouth," "Formerly a Slave," "The House-Top," and "Chattanooga" instantly create admirers. In an appendix, he implores Northerners to sympathize with Reconstruction. *Clarel* (1876) is a very long, engaging but uneven search for religion set in the Holy Land, which he toured in 1857. In it a young American student of religion named Clarel meets and becomes enamoured of Ruth, a Zionist, to whom he describes his pilgrimage. His fellow travelers include a sceptical Jew, an easy-going Anglican clergyman, and a morally and aesthetically great man who does not act on behalf of his own beliefs (this last character, Derwent, is said to have been based on Hawthorne). In this century it has been regarded as more of a curiosity than a literary tour-de-force, and no one has wished it longer than its current five hundred pages of tetrameter couplets. Before his death *John Marr and Other Sailors* (1888) and *Timoleon* (1891) appeared. His last three books of poetry were privately published.

Melville married Elizabeth Shaw in 1847 and moved to Manhattan with her that year. Three years later they moved to the Berkshires where Hawthorne, whom he met in Pittsfield, Massachusetts, at a picnic the same year, was his neighbor. Melville had a life-long affection for Hawthorne, and his anonymous "Hawthorne and his Mosses" honors the author he would soon befriend with both a comparison to Shakespeare and the unbridled praise of being representative of the highest American talent. He had two sons and two daughters. The daughters outlived Melville but the sons died before him; Malcolm, the elder, committed suicide in 1867 at age eighteen.

Melville died at home on Twenty-sixth street, New York, of heart failure, shortly after midnight on September 28, 1891. He was seventy-two years old and left his wife and two daughters, Mrs. M. B. Thomas and Miss Melville. More than three decades earlier, his last novel, *The Confidence-Man*, had been published. At the time of his death he had become virtually forgotten except by small, admiring circles in Great Britain and the United States. In fact, a year before his death, Edward W. Bok, a columnist, even surmised that many of those who could remember Melville believed him to have already died years before. Melville is buried next to his wife, Elizabeth Shaw, in Woodlawn Cemetery, Bronx, New York. ❀

Plot Summary of
"Bartley, the Scrivener: A Story of Wall Street"

"Bartleby, The Scrivener" was first published in serial form in *Putnam's* magazine in November and December of 1853; three years later, it was anthologized in Melville's *Piazza Tales*. It is a first-person account of a relationship between the narrator (a lawyer) and the title character, an extraordinary copyist in his employment. The relationship exceeds the normal expectations and patterns of the narrator's life, thus providing his impetus for telling the intriguing story. The old, complacent Wall Street lawyer recounts his acquaintance with Bartleby, whom he has hired to copy law documents. Whenever asked to do something beyond that duty Bartleby declares "I would prefer not to," and the narrator, fascinated by his recalcitrance, tries everything in his power to get him to work, but fails. Instead of evicting Bartleby he moves offices elsewhere. Bartleby dies in the Tombs, a Manhattan prison, and the narrator laments for him and for all of humanity in the story's melodramatic last line. While today it is widely anthologized and second in popularity among Melville's shorter writings only to *Billy Budd,* during its time it was ignored. In the reviews of the summer of 1856, "The Encantadas" and "Benito Cereno" were the two tales most ecstatically praised.

The lawyer specializes in drawing up legal documents such as bonds and deeds for robber barons, and a few years before Bartleby's entrance into his chambers he had been Master of Chancery, a post he laments having lost due to a change in the Constitution. His gloomy Wall Street office is surrounded by two walls: one is an interior white wall of a skylight shaft and the other is an outside brick wall ten feet away. While the chambers seem to be dim, claustrophobic, and as crowded as any Manhattan law firm today, he has a wonderfully shrewd sense of humor about them and about his general circumstances. His resentment at his tedious work does not extend to the tone of his narration, which is filled with the self-consciousness, excitement, and irony of a captivating storyteller.

Needing a third copyist, he hires Bartleby, who joins employees called Turkey, Nippers, and Ginger Nut (these are their nicknames; we are never given the "real" names of anyone except Bartleby). A stout, English, temperamental man about sixty years old, Turkey does his best work in the mornings, before his noon meal. In the afternoons he is careless, spastic, and prone to spilling blots of ink on the documents on his desk, a practice that excessively irritates the lawyer, who cannot succeed in giving him either winter outerwear or the afternoons off. Nippers is half his age, and is most productive in the afternoons, once he has finished obsessively grinding his teeth and adjusting his desk. Much of the lawyer's time is occupied in skillfully using their services at the right times. Ginger Nut is a young errand-boy.

Bartleby remains the center of his attention. He fast becomes the narrator's most competent scrivener, or copyist, but almost immediately starts to display odd mannerisms: first, he refuses to check his copying for errors with the other copyists, nonchalantly uttering his enigmatic "I would prefer not to," an answer he then proceeds to give to all the narrator's requests. When asked to assist in urgent tasks besides copying, Bartleby never consents, and Turkey and Nippers, depending on the time of day, either tolerate or try to strangle him. The most complex reactions to Bartleby emerge from the lawyer, however, whom we continually observe finding himself caught between tragic pity for the man and fear of the control Bartleby has managed to gain over the office's operations. His curiosity about Bartleby's past, motivation, and possible hidden activities mount until he becomes a shadow of himself, gripped by the man whose passivity unnerves him, and compelled to rationalize to himself and others his preferential treatment of Bartleby. Most of the narrative consists of his tormented musings on the man whose few words and fewer actions remain incomprehensible. The mystery intensifies when, stopping by the office on a Sunday, he sees Bartleby there; he leaves, and when he returns minutes later he looks around only to discover that Bartleby has been living at the office. Filled with sorrow at what he imagines to be Bartleby's extreme loneliness, he tries to solace him, but upon learning that Bartleby stops working altogether, the narrator gives him money and six days to leave the office. Bartleby "prefers not" to leave, exceedingly vexing the lawyer, since by this point Bartleby has consumed so much of his psychological energy that his previously sympathetic thoughts turn murderous. As Bartleby lingers on in the office, becoming a center of attention for visitors, the only thing left to do is to move offices, and after they do so, Bartleby remains behind, much to the bewilderment of the building's new tenants. The lawyer pleads with him but he refuses to budge; this leads him to a mounting sense of guilty paranoia that he will be held accountable for Bartleby in the eyes of the law and popular opinion. By this point in the story his emotional life seems to have been taken over by his former copyist, as he becomes preoccupied with absolving himself of responsibility as hastily as possible.

Learning that Bartleby had been sent to the Tombs, or the city prison, the narrator visits him, and he appears resentful and refuses to eat dinner. A few days later, mysteriously, he dies, and the narrator learns that Bartleby had worked in the Dead Letter Office in Washington, but was let go after a change of administrations. This news provides yet one more impetus for a pointed expression of his obsession with charity, like his own, that cannot manage to save lives, as he concludes: "on errands of life, these letters speed to death. Ah, Bartleby! Ah, humanity!" ❀

List of Characters in
"Bartley, the Scrivener:
A Story of Wall Street"

Narrator: An elder Wall Street lawyer, formerly Master of Chancery, he enjoys a comfortable life drawing up legal documents. He is not terribly ambitious, but seems a dutiful, responsible, if not slightly vain man. While we are not given the details of his life other than those that concern Bartleby, the story itself is a fascinating study of the workings of his mind, because we constantly watch him alternate between the extremes of pity and resentment, generosity and murderous hatred.

Turkey: A stubborn, histrionic, devoted employee. Turkey is around the same age as the narrator. He has a volatile, though highly predictable, personality. In the mornings he does great copying but after lunch returns to work as if in a rage, breaking pencils and spilling ink on documents. Turkey's favorite expression, when he is calm, is "with submission, sir."

Nippers: Twenty-five years old, Nippers is Turkey's opposite, having his own vices. He is disturbingly restless in the mornings, whereas Turkey exhibits such behavior in the afternoons. He is also an enterprising young man, with visiting clients for whom he writes legal documents.

Ginger Nut: A twelve-year-old errand-boy, he is often sent by the others to obtain a ginger-nut cake, thus his nickname.

Bartleby: He joins the other two copyists as a determined and energetic worker. He refuses to do anything beyond that task, and eventually gives up copying altogether, living in the narrator's chambers long after the office has moved, until finally taken to prison where he soon dies. Whenever asked by the narrator to do odd jobs, he replies "I would prefer not to" and clings to this formula as a means of isolating himself from all requests for information or work. Bartleby is portrayed as a force that refuses to be subject to the narrator's controlling gaze or interrogation. The little that the narrator can surmise about his possessions and habits cannot serve to illuminate his psychology, and he perplexes where he most delights; some readers suggest, on the basis of his profession and his having been laid off from the Dead Letter Office, that he is an autobiographical portrait of the author; others seek to find literary (Nemo in Dickens' *Bleak House,* for example) and real-life predecessors. He remains a great original, a symbol of heroic recalcitrance in the face of persistent urgings to do other than that which he prefers. ❁

Critical Views on
"Bartley, the Scrivener: A Story of Wall Street"

LEO MARX ON BARTLEBY'S LESSON TO WRITERS

[Leo Marx, the William Kenan Professor of English at MIT, is the author of *Machine in the Garden: Technology and Pastoral Ideal in America*. In this excerpt from his article on reading the story as an allegory for Melville's situation as a writer, he meditates on Melville's sympathetic portrayal of Bartleby in relation to his fellow scriveners.]

Melville's analysis of Bartleby's predicament may be appallingly detached, but it is by no means unsympathetic. When he develops the contrast between a man like Bartleby and the typical American writers of his age there is no doubt where his sympathies lie. The other copyists in the office accept their status as wage earners. The relations between them are tinged by competitiveness—even their names, "Nippers" and "Turkey," suggest "nip and tuck." Nevertheless they are not completely satisfactory employees; they are "useful" to the lawyer only half of the time. During half of each day each writer is industrious and respectful and compliant; during the other half he tends to be recalcitrant and even mildly rebellious. But fortunately for their employer these half-men are never aggressive at the same time, and so he easily dominates them, he compels them to do the sort of writing he wants, and has them "verify the accuracy" of their work according to his standard. When Bartleby's resistance begins they characteristically waver between him and the lawyer. Half the time, in their "submissive" moods ("submission" is their favorite word as "prefer" is Bartleby's), they stand with the employer and are incensed against Bartleby, particularly when his resistance inconveniences them; the rest of the time they mildly approve of his behavior, since it expresses their own ineffectual impulses toward independence. Such are the writers which the society selects and, though not too lavishly, rewards.

One of Melville's finest touches is the way he has these compliant and representative scriveners, though they never actually enlist in Bartleby's cause, begin to echo his "prefer" without being aware of its source. So does the lawyer. "Prefer" is the nucleus of Bartleby's refrain, "I prefer not to," and it embodies the very essence of his power. It simply means "choice," but it is backed up, as it clearly is not in the case of the other copyists, by will. And it is in the strength of his will that the crucial difference between Bartleby and other writers lies. When Nippers and Turkey use the word "prefer" it is only because they are unconsciously imitating the manner, the surface vocabulary of the truly independent writer; they say "prefer," but in the course of the parable they never make any real choices. In their mouths "prefer" actually is indistinguishable from "submission"; only in Bartleby's does it stand for a genuine act of will. In fact writers like Nippers and Turkey are incapable of action, a trait carefully reserved for Bartleby, the lawyer, and the social system itself (acting through various agencies, the lawyers' clients, the landlord, and the police). Bartleby represents the only real, if ultimately ineffective, threat to society; his experience gives some support to Henry Thoreau's view that one lone intransigent man can shake the foundations of our institutions.

—Leo Marx, "Melville's Parable of the Walls," *The Sewanee Review* 61, no. 4 (Autumn 1953): pp. 602–627.

MICHAEL P. ROGIN ON CLASS WARFARE IN THE STORY

[Michael Paul Rogin is Professor of Political Science at the University of California at Berkely, where he teaches American Politics and Culture, and Political Theory. His most recent book is *Blackface, White Noise: Jewish Immigrants in the Hollywood Melting Pot.* This extract from *Subversive Genealogy: The Politics and Art of Herman Melville* (1979) evokes Bartleby's societal and professional isolation.]

Bartleby is Tocqueville's democratic individual, cut off from family, class, and community. He is "locked in the solitude of his own heart." He is the man, "himself alone," "not tied to time or place," that Tocqueville imagined as the subject of democratic art. Bartleby is alone not in nature, as Tocqueville predicted the hero of American poetry would be, but in the lonely crowd. Melville uses the paltry details of American life, which Tocqueville thought were artistically refractory, to make an aesthetic form.

The lawyer introduces his office by calling "spacious" the skylight shaft between his window and the white wall. "What landscape painters call 'life,'" he remarks, is visible through the opposing window, in the "lofty brick wall, black by age and everlasting shade; which wall required no spyglass to bring out its lurking beauties." No spyglass is needed because that wall "was pushed up to within ten feet of my window panes." As the narrator finds life and variety in the view from his office, the words Melville puts into his mouth call that space a "cistern." The narrator's feeble, novelistic efforts, Melville is pointing out, are false to reality on Wall Street.

The lawyer's attempt to humanize his environment gives Bartleby his negative power. It is not so much the scrivener's withdrawal from life that need explaining, as the way in which he draws in the narrator, the other employees, and the reader. The story hints at a social explanation for Bartleby's influence, and insists on a psychological one.

—Michael P. Rogin, "Melville and the Slavery of the North" in *Subversive Genealogy: The Politics and Art of Herman Melville* (New York: Macmillan and Company, 1983): p. 112.

Jorge Luis Borges on Melville's Anticipation of Kafka

[Argentine poet, philosopher, and fiction writer Jorge Luis Borges (1899–1986) was the winner of several international literary awards and honorary degrees. His short story collections include *Ficciones* (1944), *The Aleph* (1949), and *Dreamtigers* (1960). In the following paragraphs he writes of "Bartleby, the Scrivener" as foreshadowing Kafka's fiction.]

"Bartleby" is written in a calm, even droll diction whose deliberate application to an infamous subject matter seems to prefigure Kafka. Nevertheless, between both fictions, there is a secret, central affinity. In the former, Ahab's monomania disturbs and finally destroys all the men on the boat (in translating Melville's novel into his own view of it, Borges ignores the survival of Ishmael, the narrator of *Moby-Dick* [trans.]); in the latter, Bartleby's frank nihilism contaminates his companions and even the stolid man who tells Bartleby's story, the man who pays him for his imaginary labors. It is as if Melville had written: "It is enough that one man is irrational for others to be irrational and for the universe to be irrational." The history of the universe teems with confirmation, of this fear.

"Bartleby" belongs to the volume entitled *The Piazza Tales* (New York and London, 1856). About another narrative in that book, John Freeman observes that it could not be fully understood until Joseph Conrad published certain analogous works, almost half a century later. I would observe that the work of Kafka projects a curious, hind light on "Bartleby." "Bartleby" already defines a genre that Kafka would re-invent and quarry around 1991: the genre of fantasies of conduct and feeling or, as it is unfortunately termed today, the psychological. Beyond that, the opening pages of "Bartleby" do not foreshadow Kafka; rather, they allude to or repeat Dickens. . . . In 1849, Melville had published *Mardi,* an entangled and even unreadable novel, but one whose basic argument anticipates the obsessions and the mechanism of *The Castle, The Trial* and *Amerika:* it presents an infinite persecution across an infinite sea.

—Jorge Luis Borges, "Prologue to Herman Melville's 'Bartleby'" in *Latin American Literature and Art* 17 (Spring 1976): pp. 8–9.

⊛

Michael Clark on Language and Ignorance in the Story

[Michael Clark received his Ph.D. from University of Wisconsin-Madison and teaches English at Widener College. He is author of *Dos Passos' Early Fiction, 1912–1938* (1987) and the 1997 *Cultural Treasures of the Internet.* In the context of comparing "Bartleby" with accounts of colonial witchcraft trials, *The Confidence Man,* and Cotton Mather's *The Wonders of the Invisible World,* he poses the intriguing question of the narrator's seeming ignorance of what to do with Bartleby.]

Though until now no one has noticed the parallel between the narrator's struggle to explain Bartleby and the Puritans' persecution of the witches in Salem, a number of critics have pointed out the desperate tautology of the narrator's questions, which try to constitute their own answers even as they seek them. In his excellent article of 1965, Norman Springer noted that the "narrator's occupation, his immediate concerns and his total profession, can be seen as his attempt to make meaning where there is no meaning," and three years earlier Kingsley Widmer portrayed the specific forms of the narrator's effort as representative of a particular moment in American intellectual history:

> Bartleby reveals the confession of a decent, prudent, rational "liberal" who finds in his chambers of consciousness the incomprehensible, perverse, irrational demon of denial, and of his own denied humanity. . . . He does his best and attempts to exorcise that rebellious and infuriating image with conventional assumptions, authority, utility, legalism, religious orthodoxy, prudent charity, flight, and, at the end, sentimental reverence. . . .The attempt to wryly force benevolent American rationalism to an awareness of our forlorn and walled-in humanity provides the larger purpose of the tale.

I believe these readings are right, up to point. They correctly indicate the coercive nature of the narrator's questions, and they show how the theological concept of the invisible world had been supplanted as a disciplinary mechanism by the various modes of thought Widmer lists. But they do not ask a rather obvious question: why does the narrator fail in his exorcism of this rebel image when everyone else in the story succeeds? After all, the narrator "was not unemployed in his profession by the late John Jacob Astor," and as a lawyer he is proficient in the discourse by which Wall Street operates. Yet everyone knows what to do with Bartleby except him. The second time Bartleby refuses to proofread some legal copy, for example, the narrator is confounded: "*Why* do you refuse?" he asks, and Bartleby replies as usual, "I would prefer not to." "With any other man," the narrator claims, "I should have flown outright into a dreadful passion, scorned all further words, and thrust him ignominiously from my presence. But there was something about Bartleby that not only strangely disarmed me, but, in a wonderful manner, touched and disconcerted me. I began to reason with him." Bartleby, of course, continues to prefer not to, and the narrator calls on his clerks Turkey and Nippers: " 'Nippers' said I, 'what do *you* think of it' 'I think I should kick him out of the office," Nippers replies, it being morning and, hence, an ill-tempered time for Nippers because of his indigestion.

> —Michael Clark, "Witches and Wall Street: Possession Is Nine-Tenths of the Law" in *Texas Studies in Literature and Language* 25, no. 1 (Spring 1983): pp. 55–76. ✆

[The novelist and critic Dan McCall, well-known critically as author of *The Example of Richard Wright* (1969), teaches American literature and fiction writing at Cornell University. In this excerpt from *The Silence of Bartleby*, he discusses the failure of legal rhetoric to assist the lawyer in coping with Bartleby.]

The Lawyer is, however, quite a lawyer. He is given to what Herbert F. Smith calls "stunning examples of legal periphrasis." Smith maybe stretches a little too far when he asserts that Turkey and Nippers are *amici curiae* who "balance each other out like contrasting paragraphs on a contract," but the simile is faithful to the informing rhetoric of the story as a whole. Smith asserts that the word "prefer" is "exquisitely chosen" to suggest "bearing before" or "setting before" in the matter of consequential choice. It is also apposite to the situation of equity pleading as opposed to common law pleading." Scholars may argue over how much we should see in the Lawyer's references to "Edwards on the Will" and "Priestly on Necessity," but Smith points out that "these very philosophic sounding titles are also perfectly appropriate as legal titles, especially for the purposes of equity pleading. All one need do is accept the pun on 'will' as 'testament' and 'necessity' in its legal sense, as cause in hardship. Both terms were common to equity pleading at the time of the writing of the story." "The doctrine of assumptions" is the subject of "a bravura punning performance" in which "assume" and "assumption" occur a dozen times in two paragraphs.

In these figures of legal rhetoric we hear a man giving a formal speech and talking to himself. His legal vocabulary impedes what he wants to say, but it is all he has to say it with. A rich and impressive comedy lies in the disjunction between all the absurdly insistent legalisms and the naked human tragedy of Bartleby. The narrator's diction is highly inappropriate. Bartleby's simple declaration keeps making that abundantly clear to him. So, the more his legal vocabulary does not work, the more the narrator uses it; intensifying it is his way of raising his voice. He cannot answer "I prefer not to." So he retreats in a blizzard of legalisms. This "eminently *safe*" lawyer who tells us he "never addresses a jury" is helplessly trying to do exactly that, and the jury he addresses begins to look suspiciously like himself.

—Dan McCall, *The Silence of Bartleby* (Ithaca, N.Y.: Cornell University Press, 1889): pp. 118–19.

[Lewis Mumford (1895–1990) was a lifelong critic and magazine writer. From *Sticks and Stones* (1924) to the autobiographical *Sketches from Life* (1982), his books show the inextricability of urban, social, and aesthetic issues. Mumford's 1929 biography of Melville is considered a classic and was reprinted several times throughout this century. In this excerpt from his discussion of Bartleby, he speculates that Melville's "miserable year" of 1853, in which he was turned down for employment, his publishers lost his plates, and he wrote very little, is reflected in his characterization of Bartelby.]

Bartleby is a good story in itself: it also affords us a glimpse of Melville's own drift of mind in this miserable year: the point of the story plainly indicates Melville's present dilemma. People would admit him to their circle and give him bread and employment only if he would abandon his inner purpose: to this his answer was—I would prefer not to. By his persistence in minding his own spiritual affairs, those who might have helped him on their own terms, like Allan or his father-in-law or his Uncle Peter, inevitably became a little impatient; for in the end, they foresaw they would be obliged to throw him off, and he would find himself in prison, not in the visible prison for restraining criminals, but in the pervasive prison of dull routine and meaningless activity. When that happened there would be no use assuring him that he lived in a kindly world of blue sky and green grass. "I know where I am!"

Whether or not Melville consciously projected his own intuition of his fate, there is no doubt in my mind that, as early as 1853, he was already formulating his answer. To those kind, pragmatic friends and relatives who suggested that he go into business and make a good living, or at least write the sort of books that the public would read—it amounts to pretty much the same thing—he kept on giving one stereotyped and monotonous answer: I would prefer not to. The deadwall reverie would end in a resolution as blank and forbidding as the wall that faced him: a bleak face, a tight wounded mouth, the little blue eyes more dim, remote, and obstinate than ever: I would prefer not to!

—Lewis Mumford, "Melville's Miserable Years" in *Herman Melville* (New York: Harcourt Brace Jovanovich): pp. 59–60. ☙

[The following extract is taken from the introduction to a collection of Melville's short stories edited by Frederick Busch. In his introduction to the volume, Busch notes the influence of Charles Dickens' 1852 novel *Bleak House* on Melville's "Bartleby, the Scrivener."]

Published by Harper Brothers into the mid-1850s, Melville also read *Harper's* magazine, renewing his subscription in 1852. And it was in *Harper's* that Charles Dickens's *Bleak House* was published serially in America, from April 1852 to October 1853. There's little reason to doubt that Melville saw those issues, including the issues of June and July 1852, containing the chapters (X and XI) called "The Law-Writer" and "Our Dear Brother." In them, a man is shown to be very much about paper and pen and, like Bartleby (at one point described as "folded up like a huge folio"), is a parody of Melville's profession.

The law copyist, or scrivener, lives in Cook's Court, near Chancery Lane. (Remember that Bartleby's employer was Master of Chancery and that, well into the mid-twentieth century, New York's Wall Street was the equivalent of London's Inns of Court.) The man who copies legal documents in *Bleak House*, Melville would have read, calls himself "Nemo, Latin for no one." An advantage cited about Nemo is "that he never wants to sleep"; he is a haunted man. His landlady says, "They say he has sold himself to the Enemy," the Devil; he is "black-humored and gloomy" and lives in a tiny room "nearly black with soot, and grease, and dirt"; his desk is "a wilderness marked with a rain of ink." "No curtain veils the darkness of the night," but Nemo's shutters are drawn; "through the two gaunt holes pierced in them, famine might be staring in. . . ." The filthy, ragged copyist, a figure of total despair, lies dead in his squalid room, the victim of an overdose of opium.

Melville, I suggest, read about Nemo before he wrote his story of Wall Street. He made Nemo his own, though he was drawn to him, I think, because the combination of despair, cruel laws, alienation, copying-out, and that "rain of ink" were irresistible. Bartleby turns his face to a dead wall because he cannot tolerate his life. In the Dickens, it is a broken heart, a lost history, a condition in life that is denied by the scrivener. In the Melville, it is human life itself that is denied. Dickens, when he drew his copyist in *Bleak House,* was angry at conditions in English life; Melville, under Dickens's influence, saw his soul as "grated to pieces" by the great chore of living.

—Herman Melville, *Billy Budd, Sailor and Other Stories.* Frederick Busch, ed. (New York: Penguin Books, 1986): pp. xi–xii.

Plot Summary of
"The Encantadas" (or "Enchanted Isles")

This group of ten sketches of the Galápagos Islands was published in March, April, and May of 1854 by *Putnam's*. It was hailed by *The Piazza Tales'* first reviewers as reminiscent of his novels including *Typee, Omoo,* and *Mardi* which had established Melville's reputation as a teller of sea tales. The sketches are generally indebted to Darwin, whose *Voyage of the Beagle* made the islands famous, Spenser's *Faerie Queene* for the epigraphs, as well as other accounts of sea voyages by Captain David Porter (*Journal of a Cruise Made to the Pacific Ocean,* 1815) and John Coulter (*Adventures in the Pacific,* 1845). In addition, Melville supplied many firsthand details from his visit to the islands as a passenger on the *Acushnet* in 1841–42. In 1832 Ecuador had taken possession, and throughout the century they were seal hunters' and whalers' favorite destination.

Thanks to the efforts of conservationists in the latter half of this century, the Galápagos that Melville describes bear little resemblance to the islands whose flora and fauna have made its ecosystem such a popular tourist spot. Melville's first sketch concerns "The Isles at Large," and two lines from its Spenserian epigraph (itself about fictional "wandering Islands") richly establish the dominant theme: "Darke, dolefull, drearie, like a greedie grave,/ That still for carrion carcases doth crave." As barren and desolate as any old, abandoned, urban factory building today, the islands are also given pathos by the extent that Melville's descriptions mirror Milton's sorrowful tone towards Satan in the character's desperately lonely soliloquies in *Paradise Lost.* As to Satan, "to them change never comes." The islands seem to have been punished for unnamed crimes; "Encantadas", the name given by the Spanish when they discovered the islands in 1535, means "bewitched" as much as "enchanted." These hideous, dreadful features characterize the island for Melville: the perpetual hissing of the island's reptiles, its "tangled" vegetation, the black, cavernous masses of rock covering the shores, and the difficulty that they present for ships trying to navigate their alternating calm air and strong currents. The second sketch focuses on the tortoises, from whom the archipelago gets its name—their black shells and yellow bellies, their hugeness, timelessness, and sturdy stubbornness. Three were brought aboard his ship, and the narrator marvels at their native environment and, finally, their deliciousness as soup.

Sketches Third and Fourth tell of Rock Rodondo and "Pisgah View." The "Round Rock" is 250 feet high. It looks from afar like a sail and permits wide views of the islands. Strange birds living in its eaves make horrid noise; penguins and pelicans dwell in its shelves. Unusual fish too easy to catch swim below. The narrator then gives the Pisgah View, locating several groups of islands, like Massafuero and Polynesia, with varying degrees of visibility from Rodondo, and finally describes the demonically volcanic, adjacent isles of Albemarle and Narborough and their Bays, known to whalers. In a mockingly serious tone, he estimates that Albemarle has a population of eleven million: including 10 million spiders, five hundred thousand of both lizards and snakes, and no men. Finally, he muses on the name of "Cowley's Enchanted Island," named by a Buccaneer fascinated by its ever-transforming shape, a creative quality the narrator associated with the poet of the same name.

The fifth sketch tells of the near loss of the frigate U.S.S. *Essex* in 1813, when its captain Porter mistook Rodondo for a sail, then upon chasing the elusive enemy watched the enemy's colors change from American to English, then disappear. Using a report from a previous traveler who sounds a lot like Melville, Sketch Sixth, "Barrington Isle, and the Buccaneers," extols the virtues of that island's tranquil landscape while imploring the audience to imagine the existence of less gruesomely violent, even sympathetic, buccaneers. The next three tales each concern particular islands—Charles's Isle, Norfolk Isle, and Hood's Isle, and the legendary figures who respectively founded them: a "Dog-King" whose subjects rebel, leaving his canine soldiers to defend him; the "Chola Widow" Hunilla; and the Hermit Oberlus. The tales of Hunilla and Oberlus are longer than any other in the collection, presenting round characters and engaging histories. Hunilla, discovered by the narrator's fellow seaman as they are about to leave Norfolk Isle, boards the ship recounting an extraordinary tale of having watched her husband and brother drown while trying out a boat after abandonment by a French captain. Her story, like that of Marianna in Melville's sketch "The Piazza," is cast in bold, Romantic tones that often become melodramatic. The narrator admires her stoicism in the face of this tragedy, especially during a return trip to the island in order to retrieve her chest, tortoise oil (the proceeds from whose later sale the captain gives Hunilla), some live tortoises, and a few dogs. Oberlus, the subject of Sketch Ninth, is the desert island hybrid of Shakespeare's Caliban and Spenser's Despair. He is the unfortunate combination of a deforming emaciation, bitterness, selfishness, corruption, and hunger for power. He grows rotten potatoes in clinker-ridden land. After ambushing a ship's crew member, for example, the stronger man reverses his fate and brings Oberlus to be whipped. Oberlus escapes, hides, and begins using a slyer, gentler tactic of seducing men to his lair, getting them drunk and transforming himself into a tyrant. Paranoid, abusive, obsessively destructive, and outrageously deceitful, he meets an end as depraved as his behavior. The delusional, monomaniacal Dog-King and Oberlus are balanced by the pathos of Hunilla.

"Runaways, Castaways, Solitaries, Grave-Stones, Etc.," Sketch Tenth, brings the tales to a close by noting the qualities of the desperate, degenerate people who find themselves on the islands (accidentally or otherwise) for extended periods of time. The difficulty of being a sailor can lead men to beach themselves, only to meet with disappointment and even insanity when negotiating the Encantadas' unyielding geography; their reversion to a barbaric, instinctual way of life is unsurprising but, as Melville skillfully reveals, it often has fascinating consequences; the barren, molten, maddening condition of the Encantadas has a unique charm and an unforgettable flavor, which cannot transcend its stubbornly fantasy-generating terrain. ❁

List of Characters in
"The Encantadas"

Narrator: The narrator of these tales at times represents a nexus of information about the Encantadas, having culled tales and pieces from sources as diverse as seamen, large histories, journalistic accounts, and his own experience. The account of Hunilla, for instance, comes from his own recollections, while the story of Oberlus is arranged from a history of the islands. His attitudes toward the islands range from bemused to scornful to terror-stricken, and often will change in the course of a sketch or two, as when the horrible, despairing description of "The Isles at Large" gives way to the amusing tortoises in the next sketch.

Dog-King: A Cuban Creole who successfully fought for Peru against Spain, he was rewarded for his valor by receiving a politically autonomous island, Charles's Isle, onto which eighty people came as subjects. He was forced to declare martial law when they rebelled and to kill some of his fellow men when their schemes became too menacing. After a confrontation between new recruits and his dogs, he was banished to Peru. The story of his rise and fall acts as a cautionary tale of the perils of amoral ambition in far-flung places.

Hunilla: Melville imbues this rare, Indian character with complexity and mystery. Widowed by a boating accident that she witnessed, she spent time counting the days after her husband's and brother's deaths. After discovery by the narrator's associate, she gives her history on the island—a French captain had left them there so that they could gather tortoise oil; he never returns for them. We are told that she has deep secrets which the narrator refuses to unfold, and his frequent exclamations of pity help to create a helpless, sad, mournful creature. For him, too, the fact that she shows little emotion when departing the island (making a final visit to the grave she dug for her husband and leaving many of her dogs behind) makes her into a restrained, proud, and resolute woman.

The Hermit Oberlus: The epigraph from the Spenserian episode of Redcrosse Knight's trip to the Cave of Despair (*Faerie Queene*, Book I) prepares the reader to meet an especially intriguing specimen of the haunting, greedy, self-consuming, abusive figure. But unlike the hermit Despair, and like the Dog-King, Oberlus' lust for power leads him to expend a startling amount of energy on exploiting those who visit the island for respite or food. As if to signal the extent of his hallucinations of grandeur, he quotes *The Tempest*'s resentful Caliban: "This island's mine by Sycorax my mother." More of the time, however, he seems Mammon-like, hoarding rotten potatoes, pumpkins, tortoise oil, money, and a near-dead rooster on his clinkers. He is a study in pure evil, though his deceptions—such as a letter he sent to a nearby island, asking for help because of unnamed abuses he had suffered— are not without a massive dose of humor. In order to keep control of his enslaved subjects, he ties them up every night and sleeps with a weapon that others were known to be able to seize and turn against him. Finally, when spotted trying to burn down a visiting ship, he is returned to the mainland, and ends up in a South American jail. The narrator seems to desire readers to sympathize with Oberlus; he is as much a product of his surroundings as his imagination. ❀

Critical Views on
"The Encantadas"

BASEM L. RA'AD ON THE LOST MANUSCRIPT

[Basem L. Ra'ad has taught at York University. In this excerpt he provides textual evidence for the argument that what is believed to be Melville's lost manuscript "The Isle of the Cross" is in fact Sketch Eighth of the story.]

Hunilla's story in Sketch Eighth is dominated by the cross as a symbol of her suffering and her endurance. The word "cross" is used five times in significant contexts (eight times if we count "crucifix" and "rack," and more if we consider less direct references). First, Melville cites the "rude cross" she planted "of withered sticks—no green ones might be had—at the head of that lonely grave" where she buried her husband, and then he reinforces the image by referring to "another cross," the invisible one of "dull anxiety and pain touching her undiscovered brother." The crosses gain further meaning as the narrator watches Hunilla bid farewell to the grave site. Here, Melville makes the point of the story by setting the quality of Hunilla's singular endurance against the desultoriness of the mound (and of life), with "the cross of withered sticks" at its head, "a bare heap of finest sand, like that unverdured heap found at the bottom of an hour-glass run out." Hunilla last appears in the semblance of a Christ "riding upon a small gray ass; and before her on the ass's shoulder, she eyed the jointed workings of the beast's armorial cross." [...]

But there is even stronger textual evidence, in the form of elisions and cryptic remarks, that Sketch Eighth was earlier subjected to a publisher's censure which forced Melville to omit parts of it. The elisions begin as Hunilla gives her account of what happened to her on the island. Note this series of elisions and the narrator's commentary:

> What present day or month it was she could not say. Time was her labyrinth, in which Hunilla was entirely lost.
> And now follows—

Against my own purposes a pause descends upon me here. One knows not whether nature doth not impose some secrecy upon him who has been privy to certain things. At least, it is to be doubted whether it be good to blazon such. If some books are deemed most baneful and their sale forbid, how then with deadlier facts, not dreams of doting men? Those whom books will hurt will not be proof against events. Events, not books, should be forbid . . .

When Hunilla—

Dire sight it is to see some silken beast long dally with a golden lizard ere she devour. More terrible, to see how feline Fate will sometimes dally with a human soul, and by a nameless magic make it repulse a sane despair with a hope which is but mad. Unwittingly I imp this cat-like thing, sporting with the heart of him who read; for if he feel not, her reads ion vain.

The implication here is that Hunilla was victimized in some way, and that the malicious acts perpetrated against her were dangerous to announce in public. Melville later gives us a clue about the nature of these acts, interspersed with more elisions:

"There were more days," said our Captain; "many, many more why did you not go on and notch them too, Hunilla?"
"Senor, ask me not."
"And meantime, did no other vessel pass the isle?"
"Nay, Senor:—but—
"You do not speak; but what, Hunilla?"
"Ask me not, Senor."
"You saw ships pass, far away; you waved to them; they passed on;—was that it, Hunilla?"
Braced against her woe, Hunilla would not, durst not trust the weakness of he tongue. Then when our Captain asked whether any whaleboats had—

But no, I will not file this thing complete for scoffing souls to quote, and call it firm proof upon their side. The half shall her remain untold. Those two unnamed events which befell Hunilla on this isle, let them abide between her and her God. In nature, as in law, it may be libelous to speak some truths.

These interruptions in the narrative strongly suggest that Hunilla was raped by a group of seamen, who then left without saving her from the island. The legal implications of such an action would have been more serious had the whalemen been American. It would have been defamatory enough to have identified a specific crew as participants in merely not saving Hunilla from her island fate. In such a case, no publisher would have been willing to add the large whaling and shipping industries to the list of Melville enemies just for the sake of truth. And the fact that the woman was Indian and Spanish may have made it more problematic to reveal the truth in public at that time. These could have been some of the reasons why Melville left the story "half" told.

—Basem L. Ra'ad, "*The Encantadas*" *and* "*The Isle of the Cross*": *Melvillean Dubieties* (Durham, N.C.: Duke University Press, 1991): pp. 317, 319–20.

☙

EDGAR A. DRYDEN ON LITERARY ECHOES IN THE STORY

[Edgar A. Dryden chairs the English Department at the University of Arizona. He is author of *Melville's Thematics of Form* and *Nathaniel Hawthorne: The Poetics of Enchantment*. This excerpt discusses Melville's ironic use of Spenser and the Biblical Mount in Sketch Fourth.]

"Sketch Third, Rock Rodondo" is structured by a familiar conflict between appearance and reality as the narrator discusses the enchantment that caused the rock to be mistaken for a sail, as well as the process whereby the "enchanted frigate is transformed apace into a craggy keep." Set against the "victimized confidence" of "other voyagers" who are "taking oaths" that Rock Rodondo is a "glad populous ship," is the disenchanted view of narrator and reader who know it to be a "dead desert rock." In a world of "ocular deceptions and mirages," however, such clear distinctions are difficult to sustain, and a disturbing uncertainty begins to assert itself as the narrator leads the reader up Rock Rodondo. "How we get there, we alone know." The title and epigraph of "Sketch Fourth, A Pisgah View from the Rock" seem to establish a series of ironic contrasts by setting the visions of ideal worlds against that of a "land, not of cakes, but of clinkers, not of streams of sparkling water, but arrested torrents of tormented lava." The title, of course, refers to Moses' vision of Palestine from the top of Mount Pisgah, and the Spenserian epigraph describes the Red Crosse Knight's experience in the House of Holinesse as he was led up the Mount of Contemplation by "an aged holy man" and shown a vision of "New Hieriusalem." In Spenser, the lines immediately following Melville's citation link the Mount of Contemplation with Mount Sinai, the Mount of Olives, and Parnassus, a chain of associations that would have caught Melville's eye. We know from Pierre that he identifies divine speech and prophetic vision with mountain tops. There he links the "majestic mountain Greylock," ironic source of his artistic vision, with Mount Sinai, meeting place of God and Moses; with the divine mount that was the site of Christ's famous sermon; and with Bunyan's Delectable Mountains, from which the celestial city may be seen. Moses and Christ are then linked to other imposter philosophers who pretend that they are able to get a voice out of silence and to discover the Talismanic secret that will reconcile man with the world. Melville, in short, is deeply suspicious of Pisgah views, and in his world high places are often linked to deliberate attempts to blind and deceive. There is no doubt, of course, that Melville in this sketch is emphasizing the radical difference between the world as seen from Rock Rodondo and the promised worlds of the Old and New Testaments. But he is doing more than that. The world the narrator shows us is "grim and charred," but it is also enchanted, indeed in the case of Cowley's Enchanted Isle, doubly enchanted. And the "spell within a spell involved by this particular designation" suggests uncertainties that cloud the clear distinction between a fallen world and promised lands. "Self-transforming and bemocking," this isle appears in many forms, "one moment as a great city," and another as a "ruined fortification." That is to say the isle can generate both the fallen and the Pisgah perspectives, one no less deceptive than the other.

—Edgar A. Dryden, *From the Piazza to the Enchanted Isles: Melville's Textual Rovings* (Montgomery, Ala.: University of Alabama Press, 1985): pp. 62–63.

DARRYL HATTENHAUER ON AMBIGUITIES OF TIME IN "THE ENCANTADAS"

[Darryl Hattenhauer teaches contemporary American fiction at the College of Arts and Sciences, Arizona State University, where he is Associate Professor of American Studies. His dissertation, completed at University of Minnesota, was on Melville. He has also taught at Bemidji State University.]

He further confuses the chronology of time by making it impossible to tell whether the islands are postlapsarian or prelapsarian. On the one hand, they seem plainly postlapsaria: "In no world but a fallen one could such lands exist." And later, "Apples of Sodom, after touching, seem these isles." On the other hand, they also seem plainly prelapsarian. The isles look like a New World, a new virgin land for the immigrants, who will bring historical change to these isles, which have been without human history. If the islands appear to exist at the start of time, they also appear to exist during the apocalypse at the end of time. Melville suggests that the Encantadas look like the world shall look after global fire. They look "much as the world at large might, after a penal conflagration."

Past and present telescope into each other in yet another way. From the top of Rock Rodondo, the narrator reacts to the view: "Does any balloonist, does the outlooking man in the moon, take a broader view of space? Much thus, one fancies, looks the universe from Milton's celestial battlements. A boundless watery Kentucky. Here Daniel Boone would have dwelt content." This feeling of the ever-present past includes figures from the past in the narrator's present. The balloonist, a figure of Melville's present; Boone, a figure from the colonial and early national frontier movement; Milton, a Puritan and one of Melville's influences; and the man in the moon, who existed from the beginning and still does—all of these faces from different times peer simultaneously from Rodondo. In the linear-progressive view of time, we normally conceive of historical personages as existing in the line of ancestors who prefigure the present; then we would perceive Milton as standing in that long line about two hundred years away from Melville. Our depth perspective would make the people in the line shorter the farther back in time they stand. But Melville's ever-present past puts Boone and Milton not far away on a line leading away through space, but side by side in the present. Just like the man in the moon, they exist in the present, still exerting their influence, but also in the past, prefigured by their predecessors just as they prefigure their successors. Time and space collapse together: if Milton is part of the ever-present past, he is part of the present landscape; he stands next to Boone, not far away on the horizon. Likewise, the Dog-King's pilgrims recapitulate not only the Puritans who established the dominant culture of New England, but also the saving remnant of Noah's ark. Melville calls the Dog-King the "Nimrod King," who was Noah's grandson. So we have the man in the moon, Noah, Nimrod, Milton, Boone, a balloonist, and Salvator R. Tarnmoor, the pseudonymous narrator, standing in a line which has no depth dimension. Thus, they appear to stand shoulder-to-shoulder in an ever-present timelessness. Melville thereby symbolizes the New World's connection with the past, with the eternal human condition, the sinful brotherhood of humankind. The horizontal line loses its depth dimension: the past snaps back to the present, from a horizontal line to a circle, like a rubber band. Timelessness in this sense is really timefulness: it connects the present to the eternal, ever-present past.

—Darryl Hattenhauer, "Ambiguities of Time in Melville's 'The Encantadas'" in *American Transcendental Quarterly* 56, no. 3 (March 1985): pp. 6–7.

⊛

MARGARET YARINA ON THE STORY'S FALSE SURMISES

[Margaret Yarina teaches Gothic literature at Marywood College in Pennsylvania. In the following selection she discusses the false surmises that the story, from its beginning, invites its reader to make.]

In the general introduction even the initial paragraph serves most ingeniously to illustrate Melville's method of thwarting the reader's expectation of what is to follow. Scanning the description of the islands as "five-and-twenty heaps of cinders dumped here and there in an outside city lot," the reader may justifiably assume that Melville will promptly digress from a subject that he has taken pains to introduce so unattractively. No sooner has the reader drawn this conclusion, however, than he turns the page and realizes that the description of the apparently repulsive islands extends for no less than sixty-five additional pages. Then, if the next few paragraphs seem to suggest that Melville will devote the sketches of the islands entirely to the qualities he enumerates—their solitariness, their uninhabitableness, their changelessness, their desolation—yet another illusion is temporarily imposed on the reader, for by the end of the work it has been clearly shown that the islands are by no means so absolute in any of these characteristics. Their solitude has been repeatedly broken by the many people who have come to them, willingly or unwillingly; their habitableness has been proved by the fact that all these visitors have managed to survive, albeit poorly, on what the islands naturally provide. Their changelessness is more apparent than real, for although Melville states that "to them change never comes; neither the change of seasons nor of sorrow," we later find that the islands are actually in a state of the most violent geological transition, thanks to their many volcanoes; that their seasons alter, if not with rain, at least with a nightly supply of life-sustaining dew; and that their psychic climate, or "sorrow," vibrates in violent harmony with the emotions of such varied inhabitants as Hunilla, the Dog-King, Oberlus and the buccaneers. Almost as if to justify such subsequent contradictions of his introduction to the island, Melville warns, "Nay, such is the vividness of my memory, or the magic of my fancy, that I know not whether I am not the occasional victim of optical delusion concerning the Galapagos." By thus underscoring the already established impression of ambiguity and contradiction in his narrative, he seems to suggest that the reader must assume for himself the task of separating fact from fantasy in what he is told, if, indeed, such separation is humanly possible.

Further on in the introduction to the islands, Melville continues to play on the elusive qualities of the terrain he is trying to describe by mentioning that the shifting currents surrounding the islands convey an "apparent fleetingness and unreality of the locality of the isles." When he adds that "however wavering their place may seem by reason of the currents, they themselves, at least to one upon the shore, appear invariably the same: fixed, cast, glued into the very body of cadaverous death," the reader must note the explicit qualifications in what might have been a simple statement of fact. Words like "appear" and "seem" and "apparent" inject a note of uncertainty into these and many other of the most significant things Melville says about the Encantadas, and he goes so far as to hint that the character of the islands derives as much from the imaginations of their observers as from their essential being; so it is that the buccaneer Cowley (a name with appropriately metaphysical overtones in a work so metaphysical in literary style) names one of the islands after himself, suggesting, says Melville, "the possibility that it conveyed to him some meditative image of himself." Once these clear warning of subjectivity have been sounded, all that is said about the islands must be weighed carefully for ambiguity, distortion, contradiction and paradox. Just as the Galapagos current "runs at times with a singular force, shifting, too, with as singular a caprice," so runs the imagination of Melville, disdaining a monistic forward surge in favor of limitless speculative eddies, which, in their dualistic affirmation and negations, reinforce the eternal, tidal shifting of the ocean that surrounds the enchanted islands.

—Margaret Yarina, "The Dualistic Vision of Herman Melville's 'The Encantadas'" in *The Journal of Narrative Technique* 3 (1973): pp. 143–44.

☙

I. NEWBERY ON THE STORY'S AMBIGUOUS STRUCTURE

[In this excerpt, Newbery traces the circles of evil on Rock Rodondo.]

The world as surveyed from Rock Rodondo in Sketch Four is zoned into various circles, reminiscent of Dante's *Inferno* according to the influence and sway of evil. There are clearly three circles: there is the innermost heart of the island group, Albemarle and Narborough; next, a semihabitable outer ring, comprising Barrington, Charles, Norfolk, and Hood's isles; and lastly the outside world, Quito, the Polynesian chain, Kingsmill, and the Antarctic Pole. These factual geographical features, however, are adapted to the moral vision apparent throughout "The Encantadas." Thus, in the very center of the Encantadas is a volcano where "demons of fire toil" and "throw their spectral illumination for miles and miles around." From here the immutable evil curse originates. But although the crowning curse of this center is the fact that no change will ever come to it—a fact which would have cut the cycle rather short—an element of movement is introduced into the sequence of sketches by showing the power of evil diminishing in the fringe areas. To return to the image of the various rings, around the "fixed, glued embodiment of cadaverous death" which cannot support any life except that of reptiles or visiting sea birds, a ring of diminishing suzerainty spreads, surrounding the first and separated from it by malicious currents and strange delusions (the second meaning of "enchantment"). This is the second ring where the life-destroying forces of Narborough have lost some their power, so that the islands are beginning to be semihabitable. Yet with the entry of man in this only semi-bewitched world, another even more diabolical curse operates. Evil circumstances and human corruption now weave a destiny which make the inhospitable islands into a new hell, in which man's efforts to establish a society (Dog-King), a family (Hunilla), and finally a "hermitage" (Oberlus) are doomed to failure.

—I. Newbery, "'The Encantadas': Melville's Inferno" in *American Literature* (New York: Hendricks House, 1948): pp. 58–59.

YVOR WINTERS ON THE PATHETIC CHARACTER OF HUNILLA

[Yvor Winters (1900–1968) taught at Stanford after 1928. He was a poet as well as a critic who was committed to a formal, moral, controlled classicism, and his studies of literature include *Primitivism and Decadence* (1937) and *In Defense of Reason* (1947). In this excerpt he discusses the story's central themes and its most pathetic character, Hunilla.]

In "The Encantadas," we have a series of ten sketches, descriptive of the Galápagos Islands. These islands, as described by Melville, are more of the sea, as the sea appears in *Moby Dick*, than is any other land. In the first place they are so surrounded by treacherous calms and ocean currents, that for many years their exact location was wrongly charted, two groups of islands at a considerable distance apart having been charted instead of one, it was this mysterious quality which gave them their early name, *The Enchanted Islands*.

Further, of all land they are the most barren, according to Melville, and the most hostile to humans. They are inhabited only by reptiles and by seabirds, and one or two of them by the most desperate and debased of human renegades.

Melville's descriptive power in this series is at its best; the islands in all their barren archaic horror are realized unforgettably. The climax of the series is the account of Hunilla, the Chola, who went to the islands with her husband and her brother to gather turtle oil, much as the Nantucketers went to sea for the oil of the whale. Her husband and her brother were drowned while fishing. The ship that left them did not return. She was ravished by the boat-crews of two whalers and left behind by them, and was ultimately rescued and returned to Peru by the ship of which Melville was one of the seamen. She was thus a victim of the sea; that is, of brute chance and brutal malice, forces over which she had no control, and in the face of which the only supporting virtues were absolute humility and absolute fortitude: "The last seen of the lone Hunilla she was passing into Payta town, riding upon a small gray ass; and before her on the man's shoulders, she eyed the jointed workings of the beast's memorial cross."

— Yvor Winters, *In Defense of Reason* (New York: The Swallow Press and William Morrow & Company, 1947): pp. 222–23.

Plot Summary of
"Benito Cereno"

"Benito Cereno" is one of Melville's most politically and emotionally subtle tales of slavery, reminiscent of his abolitionism in *Mardi*. Written in 1855, it is based on a true story found in Captain Amasa Delano's travel narrative, published in 1817. A third-person narrative, unlike "Bartleby" and "The Encantadas," the story recounts an encounter at sea, near Chile, between Captain Delano and the title character. While the events took place in 1805, Melville sets the story in 1799. It is a difficult, unflinching account of the consequences of slavery for those involved in the slaves' maritime transportation. Delano boards Cereno's ship, the *San Dominick* (whose name Melville changed from *Tryal* to remind readers of the revolution in Santa Domingo) in order to offer assistance to Cereno, who tells his rescuer that he has lost many of his original crew members and slaves aboard his ship due to storm and disease. He also receives help from a black servant, Babo, without whom he is too feeble to carry out his command. Delano sees and is made uncomfortable by the disorderliness of the slaves, but remains inscrutably aloof during their conversation, wavering between acceptance of and skepticism towards Cereno's story. After following Delano to his boat, causing a near-fatal slave attack, near the end of the story we discover that prior to the encounter, Babo had led them to mutiny, and that during Delano's visit they had already achieved power and were only pretending to be obedient. Delano takes the slave ship to Lima, where Babo is executed, and after a brief stay at a monastery Cereno dies. Several legal depositions follow the narrative.

At the story's beginning we are immediately enveloped in the grayness of the harbor atmosphere in which the ships sit and their captains meet. Sky, sea, and fowl are ominously calm and pale: "shadows present, foreshadowing shadows to come." Cool detachment and strong misperception characterize Delano's observation of Cereno's ship arriving in the harbor, its movements being uncertain and strange. He thinks, for example, that there are monks on the ship, seeing it as a moving European monastery. Soon he realizes the figures are slaves and that the ship badly needs cleaning and repair.

He imaginatively endows it with a glorious past to account for its present state of decay.

Boarding the ship, Delano finds himself ensconced in a crowd of many blacks and few whites. They unburden onto him tales of affliction by disease, storm, and starvation. Delano's behavior is most peculiar, wavering between kindness and hostility, the latter manner formed as a reaction to Cereno's seeming irritability and tiresome weakness (almost comically, Cereno has coughing fits, for example, every time he is asked a pointed question whose answer would reveal something crucial about his ship's condition). Delano often stands aloof, although he does perform a gesture of generosity in sending for food from his ship, and sometimes he is capable of sympathizing with the captain's seeming weakness, attributing it to his unfortunate experiences. ("Seeming" is a crucial word which recurs throughout the story, like two other phrases suggesting differences between surface and reality: "appearing" and "as if.") In addition to his fluctuating stance, his work of interpretation is unusually difficult because his first impressions are often wrong, and he constantly needs to readjust his beliefs to fit the truths he discovers. The "monastery-ship" instance mentioned above is one example, and numerous others follow. He interprets the overly attentive assistance of Cereno's servant, Babo, as a sign of genuine care. Finally, Delano's own beliefs, when not factually wrong, are often repulsive. Delano's racist leanings come through in his frequent praising the submissiveness of blacks like the servant, and his obsession with captains' power. The narrator shows his own distaste for Delano when mentioning details like these, and when he stages the captains' contrasting nationalities. Delano is irked by Cereno's "Spanish" airs and reserve toward others, though Delano's own eagerness is constantly being degraded by the narrator as American, the openness of an Emersonian sensibility. The Massachusetts native more continually is subject to moral scrutiny, since many of his observations are erroneous, rash, and naive. He is keen on identifying situations as familiar but does not realize the inherent limitations of his methods. This makes him unreliable as a character, and the audience must be mindful of his errors.

The story Cereno tells him about the ship's history corroborates the slaves' reports, so Delano's suspicions of discrepancies, despite his seeing whispering sailors everywhere, cease. He continues to witness odd events, however, such as the ceremony of a chained black man ascending the poop, and refusing to ask pardon for unnamed crimes from Cereno. This has been going on every two hours for sixty days, and the man in chains, Atufal, was reputed to have been a king in his own homeland. He also sees a black man stab a Spaniard in the head with a knife and make him bleed profusely, with no reprimand, and witnesses two men trample a third man. Then Cereno leaves Delano to rest a while, and Delano explores the ship, seeing women and children, men at work. A strange incident occurs when he is given a knot from an old sailor who asks him to cut it, then is approached by a black man who takes it and throws it into the sea. Finally, Cereno returns to him, just as Delano's ship with relief food, cider, and water comes in. Afterward, descending into Cereno's cabin, Delano questions him about the extraordinary length of time it took him to get from Cape Horn to their present location. In reply Cereno so praises the blacks on board that he seems to protest too much, but Delano brushes away, once again, any sinister implications. It is a tense moment because while Delano fires questions Babo is shaving Cereno, who gets so excited by the examination that he causes himself to be cut. Supposedly in retaliation, Cereno cuts Babo's cheek. So many violent moments erupt, like this, only to be assimilated into the strange atmosphere of the ship.

The promise of a change in circumstance seems to arise when a breeze comes, and Delano seizes control, ordering the ship to be sailed inland. Delano boards his own boat, and at the instant it moves away from Cereno, the pale, weak captain suddenly lunges at him; sailors and Babo jump into the water after him. Babo puts a knife at Delano's throat upon being rescued by him and is thrown into the vessel's bottom, at which point he tries to stab Cereno. A riot ensues. Delano, horrified, realizes that his friend Aranda, the owner of the slaves who had been on board the *San Dominick,* had been murdered and did not die of disease, as he had previously been led to believe. Delano wants to chase down the ship with the mutineers on it, now making its way from the bay, but Cereno advises him against it; Delano sends a boat, promises its sailors booty, and they attack with bullets while the blacks retaliate with hatchets. The mutinous ship loses its leaders, including Atufal. Finally after much fighting, the ships are brought to Lima where a legal investigation takes place. Cereno, a mere twenty-nine years old at his deposition, stays in a monastery for the remainder of his life.

The documents from the case are appended as the final section of the story. Whatever the author's attitude towards Cereno, clearly Melville's attitude towards slavery emerges in the text. A concise, eloquent articulation of his views can be found in his ecphrastic poem, "Formerly a Slave," written in 1865: "The sufferance of her race is shown,/And retrospect of life,/ Which now too late deliverance dawns upon;/ Yet she is not at strife." ❀

List of Characters in
"Benito Cereno"

Captain Amasa Delano: From Duxbury, Massachusetts, this commander of the *Bachelor's Delight* (*Perseverance* the ship's name in the actual 1805 incident that the story is based on) boards Cereno's ship and spends a harrowing day with him that the story recounts. Critical opinion on his representation is extremely divided—some hold that he is the type of the Southern plantation owner, others cast him as an intellectualizing Northerner. His ideas about his environment and the blacks' behavior on the ship are repeatedly proven to be wrong (reading courtesy for true obedience, and sullen behavior for animosity). His persistent interrogations of the inconsistent facts given him by Cereno about the "storm" at sea (which turned out to be a slave rebellion), however, demonstrate that he is capable of some insight. His social views are horribly racist; Delano cannot understand why the Negroes would protest slavery, and he thinks that they are "naturally" inclined to exploitation. Whatever our attitude toward him, it is clear that he learns nothing about human suffering as a result of his experiences on the ship, as an observer of both the men and Cereno.

Benito Cereno: A young Spaniard, captain of the *San Dominick*, he frequently falls ill, fainting into the arms of his servant Babo, whenever he tells the story of his misfortunes on the ship. At first he tells Delano that his crew was lost through plague and storm, and he never actually tells Delano the truth of the uprising. His boldest, most self-serving action occurs towards the end of the story when, after repeated refusals, he leaps onto Delano's ship with him, risking both lives. When Delano suggests that the ordeal can be put behind him, asking "what has cast such a shadow upon you?" Cereno enigmatically replies, "the negro." He is a tormented man.

Babo: Babo appears to Delano as a perfect specimen of the docile, accommodating, black servant. If readers were not so heavily cautioned not to adopt his views, we might agree with him after witnessing Babo's attentive behavior towards Cereno. He is there to catch every fall, support every step, and he faithfully fulfills Cereno's personal needs. Later it is revealed in the legal documents that Delano had been deceived, Babo actually having led the slave revolt. ❀

Critical Views on
"Benito Cereno"

Eric J. Sundquist on Melville's Inscrutable
Characters

[Eric J. Sundquist was for many years a professor of American literature at UCLA and in 1997 he was made Dean of
the College of Arts and Sciences at Northwestern University.
He has written many critical studies, including *The Ham-
mers of Creation: Folk Culture in Modern African-American
Fiction* (1992) and *To Wake the Nations: Race in the Making
of American Literature* (1993). In this excerpt from an article
on the story, he discusses the permeability of identity and
its inscrutable boundaries, with respect to Benito and
Delano.]

"Benito Cereno," like "Bartleby" before it and *Billy Budd* after it,
depicts the incipient and perilous merger of selves, the lawyer with
Bartleby, Vere with Billy, and to a less evident extent, Delano with
Benito Cereno. Bartleby's employer and Vere, in their fathoming of
the mysterious regions of guilt to which they are exposed but for
which they are not clearly culpable, become slowly enveloped in the
tragedies of their titular characters, merging in sacrificial wastage
with victims whose innocence and impenetrable passivity offer no
handle for retort. The final tragedy of "Benito Cereno," in an irony
verging upon tautology, depends on the fact that Delano in the end
refuses or is unable to identify with Don Benito; but it is nonetheless
the case that the mystery tale brings them into close approximation
in a way that is all the more powerful in that it is virtually unconscious. We have noted that the "involuntary" character Freud
ascribes to the process of joking defines it as a partially unconscious
action and in conjunction with the naïve, the humor of empty inten-
tion, that it thus clarifies the frustrating comedy which the interplay
between Delano and the narrator produces. There is a further conjunction that defines the narrator's "dictation" of Delano's character
in the fact that, just as the flawed signals presented to him promote
"antic conceits" and trains of "involuntary suspicion" springing
unconsciously into the narrative voice, so his response to Cereno in
scenes which present no handle for retort often takes the form of

unconscious or barely intended mimicry. He becomes at one point, for example, "involuntarily almost as rude" as Don Benito; begins more and more to respond with coldness and reserve to the Spaniard's own apparently ill-bred reticence; is overcome by the "dreamy inquietude" and "morbid effect" of the mysterious calm; and at extremity feels himself the victim of some sort of recurrent "ague" or "malady" that he strives to get rid of by "ignoring the symptoms." Cereno's "black vapors" seem slowly and surely to have infected Delano, bringing him involuntarily closer to the posture of the ruined captain and to the "disease" that the revolt, like the "contagious fever" of mutiny in *Billy Budd*, itself represents—a disease that many Americans in 1855 might well have tried to get rid of by ignoring the symptoms.

—Sundquist, Eric J., "Suspense and Tautology in 'Benito Cereno'" in *Glyph: Johns Hopkins Textual Studies* 8, no. 8 (August 1981): pp. 100–101.

⚘

Dennis Pahl on Delano's Interpretive Difficulties

[Dennis Pahl works at Long Island University as an Assistant Professor. He has authored *Architects of the Abyss: The Indeterminate Fictions of Poe, Hawthorne, and Melville* (1989). In this excerpt he discusses Delano's inability to create coherent meanings out of the chaotic signs surrounding him on the ship.]

Yet while Delano may try to reassure himself about the stability of what he discerns as his historically and morally advanced position, Melville's ironic text is constantly putting into question the very basis of Delano's authority, of his sense of historical self-identity. For evident throughout is a certain *otherness within* himself that he refuses to accept, let alone acknowledge. If Delano tries to separate himself as much as possible from the increasingly bizarre world he encounters, Melville's narrative nevertheless suggests ways in which Delano takes on the very aspects of that which he considers Other. Just as, for instance, the *San Dominick* is designated in Delano's mind as "the stranger," so too is Delano himself, not long after his arrival aboard the ship, referred to as a "stranger." Similarly, while

Delano earlier locates Cereno's otherness in the Spaniard's primitive belief in superstitions, the American captain is himself shown to be likewise subject to so-called primitive thinking: he is reported to feel a "ghostly dread of Don Benito," believing that amid the many "phantoms" he witnesses, Cereno is "the central hobgoblin of all." And finally, if Cereno is, from Delano's point of view, often characterized as mentally unstable, we notice a similar kind of instability manifesting itself in the otherwise stable American: Delano is often depicted as bewildered, haunted, and "Lost in . . .mazes" of thought—to the extent that at one moment he hallucinates that he is a "prisoner in some deserted château."

No doubt an important cause of Delano's instability is the sudden sense that he can no longer trust in the usual signs that render his world both meaningful and orderly. As a literalist "incapable of satire or irony," Delano reads the world as a perfectly stable system of signs that refer *naturally,* that confer upon the things of the world a purely natural identity. Thus the image of Cereno leaning on his slave—of a captain demonstrating his loss of mastery, his dependence on an Other—serves only to shatter the world of "significant symbols" to which Delano is accustomed. It suggests instead a world of appearances, where all signs, while they are capable of being manipulated by a will to power, are nevertheless empty in themselves—as empty as the "artificially stiffened" scabbard that is supposed to hold Cereno's silver-mounted sword, the "apparent symbol of despotic command." Without a world of naturally grounded signs to rely upon, Delano is in jeopardy of losing his bearings, that is, of losing his sense of himself as a "center," as a "master" of his world.

—Dennis Pahl, "The Gaze of History in 'Benito Cereno'" in *Studies in Short Fiction* 32, no. 2 (February 1995): pp. 176–77.

[Gavin Jones's article discusses the different knowledge of languages among the narrator, Delano, Cereno, and the blacks on board the ship. In this excerpt he discusses the conflation of silence and blackness which slavery implies.]

The linguistic logic of the tale critiques the demeaning discourse of primitivism imposed by the European (or the European-American) upon the African: the tendency to view blackness as a sign of stupidity, and to create what Frederick Douglass called the voiceless condition of the enslaved. The figurative language of the tale plays a central part in this critique. The particular correlation of muteness and blackness that dominates the descriptions of Babo—for example the African's "dusky comment of silence" during the shaving scene, or his "voiceless end" and burnt body at the end of the tale—is identical to the imagery associated with Benito Cereno. Prefiguring the "silence" and "muteness" that follow Cereno's confession that "The negro" has cast a "shadow" upon him, are a series of moments in which the muteness and silence of the Spanish captain are matched by his correspondingly "dark" and "dusked" appearance. For example when Cereno is confronted by the dark muteness of the chained Atufal, "a resentful shadow swept over his face; and, as with the sudden memory of bootless rage, his white lips glued together." At the same time as "Benito Cereno" reverses the notion that Babo is a shadowy presence of silence by revealing how the African's brain—"that hive of subtlety"—spearheads an active linguistic presence that engineers the overthrow of a colonial power, Melville's tale also silences Benito Cereno's dominant white discourse, and casts the whiteness of the Spaniard into shadowy darkness. The linguistic logic of the tale is equivocal: it tends to equate racial groups, thereby confusing the racist hierarchy upon which Delano's ideology depends.

—Gavin Jones, "Dusky Comments of Silence: Language, Race, and Herman Melville's 'Benito Cereno'" in *Studies in Short Fiction* 32, no. 1 (January 1995): p. 48.

WILLIAM BARTLEY ON INDIVIDUALISM AND DETERMINISM IN MELVILLE

[William Bartley teaches English and American literature at University of Saskatchewan, where he is Assistant Professor. In a recent discussion of the story, he illuminates Babo's haunting creation of Cereno, after shaving him.]

More significant, as Babo finishes up the shave, we see new intensities in his manner. First he massages Cereno's head with a vehemence that causes "the muscles of his face to twitch rather strangely" —a slightly Gothic and relatively clumsy touch on Melville's part. But there is nothing clumsy in what follows:

> His next operation was with comb, scissors and brush; going round and round, smoothing a curl here, clipping an unruly whisker-hair there, giving a graceful sweep to the temple-lock, with other impromptu touches evincing the hand of a master; while, like any resigned gentleman in barber's hands, Don Benito bore all, much less uneasily, at least, than he had done the razoring; indeed, he sat so pale and rigid now, that the negro seemed a Nubian sculptor finishing off a white statue-head.
>
> All being over at last, . . . the negro's warm breath blowing away any stray hair which might have lodged down his master's neck; collar and cravat readjusted; a speck of lint whisked off the velvet lapel; all this being done; backing off a little space, and pausing with an expression of subdued self-complacency, the servant for a moment surveyed his master, as, in toilet at least, the creature of his own tasteful hands.

"Creature," drawing on its root sense of "create," is anything made, and so includes the familiar, associated senses of "one who is actuated by the will of another—an instrument, a puppet—one produced by, or owes its being solely to another being," or "a person subject to the will and influence of another." Certainly by this point we are aware that Babo has made Cereno in these possessive, appropriative senses, through an artistically reductive enterprise that unfolds in the course of Babo's masquerade. But this passage discloses an extraordinary fulfillment of Babo's artistic capacity to fashion roles, a fulfillment horribly enabled by the tendency of Babo's artistry to approach the formal sensitivity, practical skill, and creative passion of the accomplished sculptor. If Babo emerges here as "a Nubian sculptor finishing off a white statue head," this has a far more ominous thematic significance than Karcher ascribes when she sees it as evoking the "artistry that recalls an African heritage of civilization, rather than of barbarism"—and thus earning its presence in the story merely as a device to counteract a crude stereotype. Instead, we can trace the convergence of that artistry with the ultimate form of might.

As a crucial point of contact in that convergence, Babo becomes a version of Pygmalion, a symbol with a wide currency in nineteenth-century American literature. And like Pygmalion, in at least one of the symbol's latent implications, Babo insists upon another human being's unconditional submission to the necessarily reductive confines of his own possessive conceptions and constructions, to the dictates of his own projected desires and hopes for the other. In Babo's case, his insistence finds its fulfillment in a species of domination that takes the appropriate metaphorical form of both fashioning and imprisoning that person in stone.

—William Bartley, "The Creature of His Own Tasteful Hands: Herman Melville's 'Benito Cereno' and the 'Empire of Might'" in *Modern Philology* 93 (1996): pp. 461–62.

☙

DIANA J. SCHAUB ON POWER RELATIONS

[Diana J. Schaub is a member of the Political Science Department at Loyola College, Maryland. Her publications include *Erotic Liberalism: Women and Revolution in Montesquieu's Persian Letters* (1995). In the following paragraphs, she takes up a much-neglected aspect of the story, that of the women's roles in the slave rebellion, and Delano's racist tendencies in relation to women and the blacks more generally.]

In "Benito Cereno," the women make one other unique contribution to the rebellion: "in the various acts of murder, they sang songs and danced—not gaily, but solemnly." The women endow revenge with a ceremonial, religious gravity. There is something horrible and bloodthirsty in their calls for torture and in their sacramentalization of murder, but there is also something righteous, something indicative of a desire for exact justice. Whereas the men are prepared to spare the captain so as to take advantage of his navigational skills, the women care more for the gratifications of revenge. They dwell more on the hurts of the past than the possibilities of the future. During the final pitched battle, the women once again "sang melancholy songs"; Melville adds that "this melancholy tone was more inflaming than a different one would have been, and was so intended." Why should woeful songs be more inspiriting than martial strains? Presumably the sorrow songs remind the men of the desperate fate of the women and children should the men fail to secure freedom.

Delano, however, intuits nothing of the women's deeper passions. All he sees is "sunny" and "sociable." When further attempts by the Spanish sailors to signal him revive his suspicions, he is again stymied by his inability to take the blacks seriously. "But if the whites had dark secrets concerning Don Benito, could then Don Benito be any way in complicity with the blacks? But they were too stupid. Besides, who ever heard of a white so far a renegade as to apostatize from his very species almost, by leaguing in against it with negroes?" Moral qualities, such as loyalty and courage, Delano is prepared to find among the blacks, but intellectual ability is ruled out and, from this passage at least, it is the possession of reason that defines the species.

—Diana J. Schaub, "Master and Man in Melville's 'Benito Cereno'" in *Poets, Princes, and Private Citizens: Literary Alternatives to Postmodern Politics* (Lanham, Md.: Rowman & Littlefield, 1996): p. 48.

DAN MCCALL ON LOWELL'S PLAY

[The novelist and critic Dan McCall, well-known critically as author of *The Example of Richard Wright* (1969), teaches American literature and fiction at Cornell University. In *The Silence of Bartleby*, he recounts watching Robert Lowell's dramatized version of the story, finding the shaving scene powerfully rendered and truthful to Melville.]

Robert Lowell adapted "Benito Cereno" to the stage as "The Old Glory," and I attended an off-Broadway performance. The curtain-raiser was Hawthorne's "My Kinsman, Major Molineux" (done wonderfully right, the actors wearing masks, the stage machinery somehow becoming the voice of the story). In Lowell's creative modulation of "Benito Cereno," the most shocking moment came when Babo shaved Don Benito: there before us was an immensely tall Don Benito Cereno, with a Spanish flag spread over him as a barber's sheet, and there was Babo in a gunny-sack loin cloth, his bright razor flicking and nicking the suds on the face of the white man. The night I saw it, the sold-out auditorium was utterly hushed, except for one middle-aged black man in the front row, almost under the scene, who got possessed of uncontrollable laughter. There was silence everywhere in the theater except for that black man's high-pitched skittering giggle. I thought Babo might "break." I thought the actor, Roscoe Lee Browne, might say something, because it was an altogether impossible situation, that silence all around us pierced by the man down in the front row, convulsed, seeing a black slave brandishing a gleaming straight razor at a white master's soapy chin. After the performance, back-stage, I saw the man from the front row standing at Roscoe Lee Browne's dressing room door. The man was apologizing, and suddenly Browne embraced him and said, "My man, don't apologize, you got the point!" The point? Whose point? Was it Melville's point back there, or is it Lowell's point now?

—Don McCall, *The Silence of Bartleby*, (Ithaca, N.Y.: Cornell University Press, 1985): pp. 66–67.

ⓒ

Charles Nnolim on the Naming of Minor Characters in the Story

[Charles Nnolim is the author and co-editor of several books on African fiction, including the 1992 *Approaches to the African Novel: Essays in Analysis.* His early book on "Benito Cereno" contains insightful essays on names and symbolism in the story; the following paragraphs discuss the significance of the names of minor characters in the story, the Spaniards Martinez and Barlow, and the recalcitrant man in chains, Atufal.]

We learn that after the capture of the *San Dominick* by Delano's men, some of the Negroes who were shackled were killed by the Spanish sailors. Two of these Spanish sailors were particularly vindictive and Melville gave them names that convey their functions in the story. Martinez and Barlo are the "hawks"—warlike figures balked of their prey. Concerning Martinez which means "Warlike," Melville says that "Captain Amaza Delano used all his authority, and, in particular with his own hand, struck down Martinez Gola, who, having found a razor in the pocket of an old jacket of his, which one of the shackled negroes had on, was aiming it at the negro's throat." The name-symbol stands out. What is more "warlike" than the act in which Martinez is caught perpetrating? That other "hawk" Barlo is equally given a name that fits his function in the story. The deposition says "that the noble Captain Amasa Delano also wrenched from the hand of Bartholomew Barlo a dagger, secreted at the time of the massacre of the whites, with which he was in the act of stabbing a shackled negro, who, the same day, with another negro, had thrown him down and jumped upon him." "Barlow" of course means "a one-bladed jack knife" or a dagger. Again, here, the name describes the character.

An important African slave who was called many times Babo's "lieutenant" deserves mention here. He is the giant Atufal who was in chains, whose key was hanging from Don Benito's neck. Atufal was a king in Africa and must have been the victim of an intertribal warfare. On sight of Atufal the awed Delano could not help exclaiming: "Upon my conscience, then, . . . he has a royal spirit in him, this fellow." "He may have some right to it," bitterly returned Don Benito, "he says he was king in his own land." Atufal and Dago were Ashantee Negroes so that the exact meaning of their names are unavailable to this study. But their function in the story are suggestive of several thematic symbols. Although James Miller thought that Atufal is a symbol of "brute strength," a more perceptive approach would seem to point at Atufal's chain as a symbol of slavery itself and the injustice and indignities consequent on it. Atufal never spoke a word in the whole tale, but the gestures attributed to him indicate that in addition to being one of the architects of the rebellion, his demeanor underlines Babo's protest to slavery. When Don Benito called him to apologize for an unspecified wrong he was accused of committing, Melville says: "Upon this, the black, slowly raising both arms, let them fall, his links clanking, his head bowed; as much as to say, 'No, I am content.'"

—Charles Nnolim, *Melville's "Benito Cereno": A Study in Meaning of Name Symbolism* (New York: New Voices Publishing Company, 1974): pp. 50–51.

Plot Summary of
Billy Budd, Sailor

Billy Budd, Sailor is the story of a handsome English sailor, aged twenty-one, who is hated for his youthful beauty by Claggart, a bitter master-at-arms acting as a kind of on-board police chief. It takes place in 1797 when Great Britain was warring with post-Revolutionary France. Billy is sailing home on the *Rights-of-Man* when it meets up with the *Bellipotent* (Latin for "war-power"), whose Lieutenant Ratcliffe is looking to forcibly impress men into service. Billy is brought on board and his trials at the hands of Claggart, the resentful, evil, jaded officer, begin. They are men of completely opposite sensibilities: one is open, innocent, and honest, and the other is worldly, disillusioned, and cruelly jealous. After failing to get someone to bribe Billy to mutiny, Claggart insinuates Billy's waywardness in Captain Vere's presence. Billy, dumbfounded, cannot speak in his own defense (he is known to stutter in moments of extreme stress) but strikes Claggart a blow so hard it kills him. Vere assembles a courtroom and Billy is hanged in front of the ship's crew. His final words are "God bless Captain Vere!"

After the ship's company echoes him, they mutter to themselves in menacing tones. Music drowns out their speech after Billy's burial, and Vere soon dies in a fight with the French *Athée* (or Atheist—the ships' names are highly symbolic). The story ends with mentions of two conflicting references to Billy's story, one a journalistic account which claims that Billy led a mutiny, and the other is a ballad for sailors that sympathizes with Billy's perspective in lines such as "O, 'tis me, not the sentence they'll suspend" and the Lycidas-like "I am sleepy, and the oozy weeds about me twist."

While the novella's plot and juxtapositions seem simple and straightforward, its characters are deeply complex, and critics who are united in hailing the work as Melville's late, elegiac masterpiece remain divided when analyzing how we are to understand Vere, Claggart, and Billy Budd.

In the beginning of the story, Billy Budd is compared by the narrator to a handsome black sailor that he saw during the 1840s, who solicits admiration for both his well-formed body and his self-possessed physical stance. Coming on the *Bellipotent*, Billy silently accepts his change of fortune, and the *Rights'* master expresses his misgivings at losing such a popular and well-loved sailor, his "jewel" and "peacemaker" who had turned a ship of quarrelers to one with camaraderie. Billy is talked of and worshiped from afar but such high praise renders him more mythological and statuesque than real. His quiet, simple demeanor makes him seem younger than he really is, and his naiveté about proprieties allows him a degree of leniency when he acts in ways unknowingly offensive.

His oblivion to those less sympathetic to his popularity and his "simple nature" are repeatedly mentioned as ominous details. His stuttering problem at times of great urgency is also a fatal flaw which will exacerbate his troubles at their most crucial moment. These characteristics also contribute to our understanding of him as a person whose intellectual faculties are less strong as his appearance. He is pretty to look upon and well-loved, but his judgment is green and innocent. The story also gathers narrative energy from the veiled homoeroticism of the crew members. Their attraction to Billy, especially Claggart's, is seen in the light of his beauty, which is so great it inspires Claggart's envy. Without the counter-weight of a detectable moral sensibility, Billy seems almost destined to fall; it is not that he is amoral, but that he cannot recognize evil.

The fatalistic quality of his story is brought out by the ways in which Claggart, the ship's master-at-arms, or police chief is able to plant doubts about Billy's character in Vere's mind, and by the fact that Billy is up against a captain who, in light of the recent mutinies on the *Nore* and at Spithead (a mere season before their voyage), wants to follow the letter of the law to create an example for his crew. Billy is the victim of this plan, and often seen by critics as a Christ-figure. And while Vere is admired by the narrator for his virtue, his love of books, and his firm mind, he is also seen, more subtly, as excessively unbending. Billy's fate is shaped by forces beyond his control. When Vere arranges a courtroom trial for Billy, the verdict in his mind unyieldingly conflicts with his belief in Billy's innocence, and his reassuring words, "I believe you," are signs that Billy's death will haunt him until his own; indeed, on his deathbed he utters Billy's name. Vere's focus on the necessary and inevitable consequences of Billy's action—capital punishment for a capital crime—comes with the cost of his own deeply conflicted conscience. The audience can remain deeply divided about him, torn between our respect for his attention to the law and frustration at his sacrifice of an innocent man. ❀

List of Characters in
Billy Budd, Sailor

Billy Budd: Twenty-one years of age, the title character is transferred from his homeward-bound *Rights of Man* to the *Bellipotent* because the latter is short of crew. He quickly makes friends among the foretopmen among whom he works. He is an illiterate orphan who loves to sing. His mild, clean good looks lead him to be compared to a Greek sculpture of Hercules, a prelapsarian Adam, and Achilles. He is so correct in his behavior and execution of his duties that he is laughed at by his more relaxed colleagues, and he fears reprimand more than death; any errors on his part are pure accidents. He is hanged for his fatal blow to Claggart during a meeting with Captain Vere, in which Claggart falsely accuses Billy of conspiring to mutiny. He is a hero to the sailors who believe that he is unfairly hanged for a crime he did not intend to commit, and, even in death, when his hanging body does not display the normal "motion" of a corpse, he remains an unusual jewel.

Claggart: When we remember that Claggart's literary ancestors include Shakespeare's Iago, Milton's Satan, and Melville's own earlier monomaniacal Captain Ahab, we realize the extent to which his character contains the shrewd, manipulative, intelligent qualities of a canonical villain (at one point he is referred to, in one of the story's several, characteristically Melvillean, definitions via negations, as "the direct reverse of a saint"). Thirty-five years of age, and "spare" as Shakespeare's untrustworthy conspirators, he has the small hands and fair complexion of a sailor unaccustomed to manual labor. He also has the physiognomy of a Restoration, Popish fraud. These details seem to cast him unfairly in a negative light, prejudging him in ways that are beyond his control. His past life before being on board is unknown, which subjects him to skepticism on the part of less charitable sailors. His occupation, preserving order on the ship, makes him unpopular.

Captain Vere: The Captain, the Honorable Edward Fairfax Vere, is a forty-year-old bachelor and eminent sailor. He is committed to discipline, order, and is serious and stoical. Tellingly, his favorite author is Montaigne, whose essays he reads to discover in them confirmations of his own deeply conservative opinions about human behavior. He is contemplative, even "dreamy," getting his nickname "starry Vere" from a line in Marvell's "Upon Appleton House" that alludes to one of his ancestors. His heavily allusive speech creates a formidable distance between himself and his crew, and the narartor attributes to his "honesty" his inability to speak in different registers. He sees to it that Billy's trial and execution proceed as rapidly as possible so as not to generate too much attention. In sentencing him, he pleads with Billy's generous understanding of his military obligations. When he stands "erect as a musket" at hearing the echo of Billy's last words, "God bless Captain Vere!", it is difficult to surmise whether he is being erotically energized by the experience or stricken nearly dead by it, even for a moment. ❀

Critical Views on
Billy Budd, Sailor

F. O. MATTHIESSEN ON SYMPATHY FOR VERE

[F. O. Matthiessen (1902–1952) was a Yale graduate and Harvard Ph.D. who taught at both institutions. He was politically liberal and very religious. His critical studies include *The Achievement of T. S. Eliot* (1935, revised 1947) and numerous books on Henry James. In *American Renaissance* (1941), his famous study of "art and expression in the age of Emerson and Whitman," he dedicates a chapter to *Billy Budd*, in which the following excerpt, on Vere's personality, appears.]

The central scene of the drama takes place in Vere's cabin. The captain has an instinctive mistrust for Claggart, but deems it necessary to summon Billy to answer the charge just brought against him. A familiar strain of Melville's imagery asserts itself as Claggart fixes Billy with his eyes, which become 'gelidly protruding like the alien eyes of certain uncatalogued creatures of the deep. The first mesmeric glance was one of surprised fascination; the last was as the hungry lurch of the torpedo-fish.' The unsuspecting sailor is so amazed by the suddenness of the accusation that he is speechless, seized by one of his paroxysms of stuttering. Desperate to break its spell and to assert his innocence, he strikes out, and the force of his blow over Claggart's temple is such that it not only fells him to the deck, but kills him. With a single insight Vere grasps the whole situation: 'Struck dead by an angel of God. Yet the angel must hang!' In the court-martial that he summons, he points out to his less intelligent and less rigorous officers that they must not let themselves be swayed by their feelings, that the recent great mutiny in the fleet will not permit now any swerving from the strictest discipline. He argues that they do not owe their allegiance to human nature, but to the king, that martial law can deal only with appearance, with the prisoner's deed; and he fears how appearances will affect the crew if a murderer is not executed. 'But I beseech you, my friends, do not take me amiss. I feel as you do for this unfortunate boy. But did he know our hearts, I take him to be that generous nature that he would feel even for us on whom in this military necessity so heavy a compulsion is laid.' Yet the heart is 'the feminine in man, and hard though it be, she must be ruled out.'

In such manner the struggle between Claggart and Billy is re-enacted on a wholly different plane within the nature of Vere himself. He has the strength of mind and the earnestness of will to dominate his instincts. He believes that in man's government, 'forms, measured forms, are everything.' But his decision to fulfil the letter of his duty is not won without anguish. He holds to it, however, and thereby Billy, who had been defenseless before the evil mind of Claggart, goes to defeat before the just mind as well. It does not occur to him to make any case at his trial. He is incapable of piecing things together, and though certain odd details that other sailors had told him about the master-at-arms now flash back into his mind, his 'erring sense of uninstructed honor' keeps him from acting what he thinks would be the part of an informer against his shipmates. So he remains silent, and puts himself entirely in his captain's hands.

—F. O. Matthiessen, *American Renaissance: Art and Expression in the Age of Emerson and Whitman* (New York: Oxford University Press, 1968): pp. 508–9.

BARBARA JOHNSON ON INTERPRETIVE DIFFICULTY IN THE STORY

[Barbara Johnson teaches English at Harvard and is the author of many critical studies including *World of Difference* (1987) and *The Wake of Deconstruction* (1994). Her popular essay on the novella is considered a classic example of critical deconstruction. In the following paragraphs she meditates on the intricate, important differences between "appearance and action," or "being versus doing" in Claggart's hostility towards Billy.]

Curiously enough, it is precisely this question of being versus doing that is brought up by the only sentence we ever see Claggart directly address to Billy Budd. When Billy accidentally spills his soup across the path of the master-at-arms, Claggart playfully replies, "Handsomely done, my lad! And handsome is as handsome *did* it, too!" The proverbial expression "handsome is as handsome does," from which this exclamation springs, posits the possibility of a continuous, predictable, transparent relationship between being and doing. It supposes that the inner goodness of Billy Budd is in harmonious accord with his fair appearance, that, as Melville writes of the stereotypical "Handsome Sailor" in the opening pages of the story, "the moral nature" is not "out of keeping with the physical make." But it is this very continuity between the physical and the moral, between appearance and action, or between being and doing, that Claggart questions in Billy Budd. He warns Captain Vere not to be taken in by Billy's physical beauty: "You have but noted his fair cheek. A mantrap may be under the ruddy-tipped daisies." Claggart indeed soon finds his suspicions confirmed with a vengeance: when he repeats his accusation in front of Billy, the master-at-arms is struck down dead. It would thus seem that to question continuity between character and action cannot be done with impunity, that fundamental questions of life and death are always surreptitiously involved.

In an effort to examine what is at stake in Claggart's accusation, it might be helpful to view the opposition between Billy and Claggart as an opposition not between innocence and guilt but between two conceptions of language, or between two types of reading. Billy seemingly represents the perfectly *motivated* sign; that is, his inner self (the signified) is considered transparently readable from the beauty of his outer self (the signifier). His "straightforward simplicity" is the very opposite of the moral obliquities or "crookedness of heart" that characterize "citified" or rhetorically sophisticated man. "To deal in double meanings and insinuations of any sort," writes Melville, "was quite foreign to his nature." In accordance with his "nature," Billy reads everything at face value, never questioning the meaning of appearances. He is dumbfounded at the Dansker's suggestion, "incomprehensible to a novice," that Claggart's very pleasantness can be interpreted as its opposite, as a sign that he is "down on" Billy Budd. To Billy, "the occasional frank air and pleasant word *went for what they purported to be,* the young sailor never having heard as yet of the 'too fair-spoken man.'" As a reader, then, Billy is symbolically as well as factually illiterate. His literal-mindedness is represented by his illiteracy because, in assuming that language can be taken at face value, he excludes the very functioning of *difference* that makes the act of reading both indispensable and undecidable.

—Barbara Johnson, "Melville's Fist: The Execution of Billy Budd" in *Studies in Romanticism* 18, no. 4 (Winter 1979): pp. 52–53.

NEAL TOLCHIN ON THE TRIANGULATION OF CLAGGART, GRIEF, AND HEALTH

[Neal Tolchin is author of *Mourning, Gender, and Creativity in the Art of Herman Melville* (1988). In this excerpt he pinpoints what is so stifling about Claggart to Melville's conception of himself as a writer.]

The novel associates Billy with instinctive, natural life, with roses, gold finches, horses, dogs, and with an infant in the cradle. Billy is also associated with creativity, as he sings and makes up his own songs. In one of his dimensions, Billy is linked to a principle of growth; he seems to personify the creative élan from which Melville was cut off soon after he completed *Moby-Dick*.

Claggart, on the other hand, in part personifies the forces that obstructed Melville's creativity. One of the forces that silenced Melville as a novelist was his family's suspicion that his writing was impairing and might permanently damage his mental health. At the crucial moment of his fatal accusation of Billy, Claggart nears him, "With the measured step and calm collected air of an asylum physician approaching in the public hall some patient beginning to show indications of a coming paroxysm."

The family suspicion of Melville's emotional stability intensified because Melville's mother turned him into a living linking object to her husband. In a sentence deleted from his manuscript, Melville observed of Claggart, "Behind these frescoed walls of flesh, it is the closeted skeleton." The crew's suspicion of Claggart as a "chevalier," who has found his way into the navy "by way of compounding for some mysterious swindle," evokes Melville's memory of the bankruptcy into which his father's underhanded business dealings plunged his family.

Claggart "looked like a man of high quality, social and moral, who for reasons of his own was keeping incog." Further, Claggart reminds Vere of a "perjurious witness in a capital case before a court-martial ashore": as such he seems the tarnished image of Melville's father brought to the bar of his son's conscience. The lingering trace of an accent in Claggart's speech links to Allan Melville's French import trade, as does Claggart's "peculiar ferreting genius." Claggart's "self-possessed and somewhat ostentatious manner" mirrors Allan's pretentious upper-class manner. When Claggart looks at Vere like Jacob's "envious children . . . deceptively imposing upon the troubled patriarch the blood-dyed coat of young Joseph," Melville evokes both the memory of the faltering coat-factory Allan left as a legacy to his family and perhaps as well his own sense of abandonment— the fate of Joseph—after his father died.

—Neal L. Tolchin, *Mourning, Gender, and Creativity in the Art of Herman Melville* (New Haven, Conn.: Yale University Press, 1988): pp. 163–64.

John Samson on Nature, Narrative, and the Story

[John Samson is author of *White Lies: Melville's Narratives of Facts* (1989). He teaches at Texas Tech University. In this excerpt he shows how conservative naval values are inculcated by the narrative's perspective on Billy's fist.]

When, therefore, Billy's fist intrudes upon Claggart's narrative, Vere, like Melville's earlier narrators of facts, has trouble fitting the act into the picture of Billy his faith has generated. In this violent act, Billy shows himself neither an Adam nor a Christ. Vere may call it "the divine judgment on Ananias" and label Billy an angel, but neither of these statements will adequately explain the violence of the attack. Even as he perceives Billy from this Christian perspective, Vere is forced to perceive Billy's actions from a military perspective as well. Thus Vere presents a dichotomy familiar to readers of the earlier narrative of facts: a dubious faith opposed and undermined by an inveterate politics. Vere, as his name might suggest, is a man of the seventeenth century (like Marvell) who can still believe these two spheres compatible, despite living in a century that explodes them. Like Melville's earlier narrators, Vere is caught in this dissociation of sensibility and must act as if "unhinged"; he chooses to place Billy's inner self within the Christian context but his outer within the political. Little wonder the surgeon suspects insanity, for such a schizophrenic determination cannot but warp Vere's perspective, create turmoil for himself, and distance him even further from reality. Indeed, the problem of Billy haunts him until his dying day.

Melville replays these conflicts in his narrator, a contextual critic who amplifies the biases, motivations, and mistakes of Vere. Further testifying to the spiritual desire behind narration, the narrator, like Vere, consistently describes Billy in mythic and Christian terms. And yet, as he tries to approach Billy through the "indirection" and "lateral light" of personal and historical precedents—and incompetently so, as Garner's study indicates—the narrator goes further than Vere. To name a few: he tells of Nelson, the Somers mutiny, the Nore case; he refers to Marvell, the Bible, Thomas Paine; he reminisces about his past and makes the events into a tragedy; he employs inappropriate metaphors, inapplicable allusions, selective detailing, imaginative reconstruction. But all to no avail: he can only "suggest" what Billy "might be like."

Like Vere's, the narrator's biases are exposed by Billy's fist. The facts of the event show Billy not like the Handsome Sailor the narrator remembers, not like a Saint Bernard, not like Christ; nevertheless, the narrator tries all the more strenuously to present Billy as a heroic Christ-figure. His motives in doing so are more self-interested than religious; for—like each of the other narrators of facts—he is using the story of Billy to justify his own conservative politics. By stressing the tragic and otherworldly aspects of Billy's story, he diverts it away from revolution and toward an acceptance of the status quo, just as Claggart uses Billy to cement his own position in the ship's hierarchy and in the captain's eyes, just as Vere uses his narrative of the story to keep order on board and to keep order in his perception of the starry system of the universe.

—John Samson, *White Lies: Melville's Narratives of Facts* (Ithaca, N.Y.: Cornell University Press, 1989): pp. 226–27.

HERSHEL PARKER ON READING THE STORY HISTORICALLY

[Hershel Parker is a textual scholar, editor, bibliographer, and interpreter of Melville's life and texts. In 1996 he published volume one of his exhaustive biography of Melville. *Reading Billy Budd* (1990) includes discussions of each chapter; the following excerpt is taken from his assessment of the opening paragraph and serves as a good example of how close attention to detail is rewarded.]

At the start of the chapter 1 qualifications almost overrun assertions. "In the time before steamships, or then more frequently than now," the story begins, locating the reader between the last decade of the eighteenth century and the "now" of the late 1880s—a stretch of some nine decades or a century—and then retreating from overassertion: if the sight to be described was not restricted to the time before steamships, at least it was more common then than now. The specified vantage point for regarding the spectacle is that of a civilian stroller along the docks, not a sailor, and the sight is that of a group of bronzed seamen flanking "some superior figure of their own class," of the type known as the "Handsome Sailor." The wording retreats from claiming the sight was witnessed in the past only "more frequently than now," for the Handsome Sailor seems to belong exclusively to that "less prosaic time alike of the military and merchant navies," the time before steamships, or at most the time not long after steamships were invented. The narrator commits himself to a belief that the present is more prosaic than the 1790s and is also more prosaic than the 1830s, for he recalls from the Liverpool of the middle past ("now half a century ago") a lustrous black Handsome Sailor he saw "under the shadow of the great dingy street-wall of Prince's Dock (an obstruction long since removed)." Wayfarers, strollers, whose attention was arrested by the barbaric son of Ham in Liverpool rendered spontaneous tributes of "a pause and stare, and less frequently an exclamation"; here "less frequently" reminds us of the opening "more frequently" in this time-saturated prose. Furthermore, the parenthetical comment about the obstruction long since removed introduces a fourth time, not only the 1790s, the late 1880s, and 1839, but also some indefinite date between the 1840s or 1850s and the present, the time when the street-wall (or, the untraveled reader may wonder, the Dock itself?) was removed. (1839 is the date of Melville's first stay at Liverpool. In a story in which the 1843 of the dedication locates Melville in autobiography and nineteenth-century history, there seems no good reason not to take the reference to Prince's Dock as autobiographical, and indeed there seems no aesthetic loss at this point if we talk of the narrator and Melville almost interchangeably.)

—Hershel Parker, *Reading Billy Budd* (Evanston, Ill.: Northwestern University Press, 1990): p. 102. ☙

[Paul McCarthy published *The Twisted Mind: Madness in
Herman Melville's Fiction* in 1990. In this selection is
described the difficulty of separating sane from insane
behavior in the novella.]

As Melville indicates in Chapter 21 and elsewhere in *Billy Budd*, distinctions between sanity and insanity are sometimes very difficult to
determine. This general view is illustrated in the case of Captain
Vere. As Melville states Vere honestly believes that because of recent
outbreaks in the British fleet at Spithead and Nore and because of
circumstances aboard the *Bellipotent* (Claggart's death in particular),
prompt action is necessary if a mutiny is to be averted. A "sense of
the urgency of the case overruled in Captain Vere every other con-
sideration." Melville makes clear also that Vere had to make his decisions in a sense "under fire"; forces beyond his control compel him
to make controversial decisions.

For once, however, the superbly dedicated and efficient officer
misreads the evidence. The surgeon and other officers are correct:
Vere is not the one to make the decision; only the admiral can make
it. Nor do the officers believe that shipboard conditions could lead
to a mutiny. Vere made mistakes in judgment because of pressures
and personal attitudes. The actions in his cabin—Billy's blow and
Claggart's death—may not be traumatic but they are nonetheless
very disturbing. Complicating the matter is Vere's admiration and
love for Billy. Vere is probably not Billy's natural father, but as shown
in cabin scenes in Chapters 19 and 21 his concern for Billy is strong
and paternal. In the private, undramatized interview with Billy in
Chapter 22 after the trial, Captain Vere is described as "old enough
to have been Billy's father." In the statement, Vere "may in end have
caught Billy to his heart," some critics see Vere's revelation of love for
Billy. Lesser writes of the relationship: "No less instinctively than he
had recoiled from Claggart's hostile assault, Billy submits to his sentence because he feels that Captain Vere has decreed it in love." In the
execution scene in Chapter 25, as Billy utters the words "God bless
Captain Vere" and the "spontaneous echo . . . voluminously
rebounded them," Captain Vere, "either through stoic self-control or

a sort of momentary paralysis induced by emotional shock, stood erectly rigid."

Despite his austere devotion to naval law, duty, and custom, Captain Vere is a vulnerable man. Brilliance and discipline fail him because the decisions about Billy and the drumhead court-martial are made on the mistaken assumption that "forms, measured forms" must always be the final standard of judgment in naval life.

—Paul McCarthy, *The Twisted Mind: Madness in Herman Melville's Fiction* (Iowa City: University of Iowa Press, 1990): p. 133.

⊗

KATHY J. PHILLIPS ON HIDDEN SIGNIFICATIONS IN THE STORY

[Kathy J. Phillips teaches English at the University of Hawaii. She is the author of *Dying Gods in Twentieth-Century Fiction* (1990) and *Virginia Woolf Against Empire* (1994). In the following selection she discusses the sexualization of warfare in Vere's attitude towards Billy.]

Moreover, Vere does not just transfer the actions of one body part onto the whole body; he also displaces phallic rigidity onto musketry. Vere then proceeds to enforce a duplicate displacement in the crew. When the sailors begin to "murmur" against the execution of the man they love, the "silver whistles" of their officers drown out the incipient mutinies of sexual, emotional, and political protest. With the effect of "an instinct," the "drumbeat dissolved the multitude, distributing most of them along the batteries of the two covered gun decks. There, as wonted, the guns' crews stood by their respective cannon erect and silent." Instead of togetherness, there is dissolution; instead of the "vocal current electric" that might have swelled mutual blessing, there is silence. Instead of openness, the men experience only more closeting and self-deception under covered decks. Instead of instinctual phallic joy, they acquire the sham instinct of a training to fire cannons automatically. The purser and the surgeon even expect to see a "muscular spasm" in Billy's body at the hanging and seem bizarrely disappointed at this absence of an erection. The discussion between these two minor characters treats the execution as a spectacle staged for the sake of their own voyeuristic kicks. Yet "to the wonder of all no motion was apparent . . . in a great ship ponderously cannoned." Instead of living, passionate, and compassionate reactions to each other, the sailors are left with only a displaced, deadly sexuality, enacted by machines and mechanized men. And as Melville's irony implies, it is really no "wonder" that cannon as phallus and hanged man as aphrodisiac are not satisfying after all.

This channeling of repressed sexuality into war takes two forms in *Billy Budd*. First, learning to deny one's own human responses makes it easier to deny the humanity of so-called enemies. Even when Vere suspects that some of the French conscripts may hold views as monarchic and undemocratic as his own, he can anticipate fighting these men with whom he has no quarrel, simply because he wears the ludicrously trivial "buttons" of Empire. If Vere and his men follow an imperial code that they do not necessarily support, he claims that "we are not responsible." According to an American professor in Europe, German students aware of the Nazi past were particularly attuned to the dangerous implications of Vere's willingness to deny responsibility.

Second, the energy that could express love, once repressed, seems to go on blindly fueling a parody of love. These soldiers need war—any war, without asking the cause—because it provides the only intensity they are allowed on that ship. If, as the students said, the name of the ship, *Bellipotent*, suggest "potent," "belligerence," and "belle," then the meaning could slide either toward "the omnipotence of war" or "the potency of the beautiful one." The story devastatingly records how denying Billy's power to arouse the other men erotically plows that energy into the killing fields.

—Kathy J. Phillips, "Billy Budd as Anti-Homophobic Text" in *College English* 56, no. 8 (December 1994): pp. 906–7.

⊕

JONATHAN ARAC ON REALISM AND HISTORY

[Jonathan Arac teaches English and critical theory at the University of Pittsburgh. His first book was *Commissioned*

Spirits: The Shaping of Social Motion in Dickens, Carlyle, Melville, and Hawthorne (1979) and in 1997 he published *Huckleberry Finn as Idol and Target: The Functions of Criticism in Our Time*. His contribution to *The Cambridge History of American Literature* (1995) includes an insightful discussion of *Billy Budd* as a realist text.]

Billy Budd is the most wholly fictional of Melville's works. It is not drawn at all directly from his experience, nor does it rework specific documents. It is set in 1797 on a British warship, and Billy is not even an American. America is no longer so unique that major work by an American writer must treat an American subject (or one with obvious bearing on the United States, such as Prescott's *Conquest of Mexico*). Parkman's history even praises the continuing spread of British colonialism in the nineteenth century, rather than treating the empire as superseded by democracy. A Britain threatened by revolutionary France might begin to seem a congenial figure for the United States. After the Civil War, slavery was ended, but other forms of social inequality increased until farmers' populism and industrial workers' agitation to unionize threatened the existing order.

Although *Billy Budd* is fiction, Melville's rhetoric is antifictional. Subtitled "An Inside Narrative," *Billy Budd* repeatedly appeals to the documentary expectations of narrative. Readers should understand that this is no "romance," and it must, therefore, lack "the symmetry of form attainable in pure fiction." Using a term not yet in the language when he began his career, Melville defends his procedures as "realism." As an inside narrative, the work corrects the news account (itself part of the fiction) of the events it recounts. In 1851, Melville had been happy to encounter a newspaper report that confirmed *Moby-Dick* by reporting a whale's sinking a ship, but now he reenacts a fundamental gesture of self-consciously innovative high culture, from William Wordsworth in the preface to *Lyrical Ballads* (1800) to Joseph Conrad in *The Secret Agent* (1907): defining the truth of one's writing by the falsity of newspapers. As "romance" had been in the 1850s, "realism" in the 1880s was the password for literary narrative.

Billy Budd performs an extraordinary historical reconstruction. It defines a limited fictional action within the juncture of important public events. These events are not just the revolutionary wars, but, specifically, the mutinies of 1797 within the British navy, and, yet more precisely, the constraints of commanding a ship detached from the fleet. Its "inside narrative" does not function like the "internal story" of *Septimius Felton* to displace attention from history to psychology. Two paragraphs from the manuscript that served as the work's preface from its first publication in 1924 until the scholarly edition of 1962 greatly enrich the complexity of historical thought by arguing that "not the wisest could have foreseen" at the time that the revolutionary excesses, or the sailors' mutiny, would eventually lead to "political advance" and "important reforms." It seems that only because they were opposed by the wisest have these movements succeeded; progress requires resistance.

—Jonathan Arac, "Narrative Forms: Crisis and Consolidation" in *The Cambridge History of American Literature*, vol. 2 (New York: Cambridge University Press, 1995): pp. 772–73.

☙

JOHN HAYDOCK ON THE INFLUENCE OF BALZAC'S *SÉRAPHITA*

[John Haydock teaches English at Hampton University. This excerpt from his article on Melville's debt to Balzac's *Séraphita* discusses the texts' shared sexual vagueness.]

Both novels also share the expression of what might be considered prominent imagery of sexual ambiguity. Séraphitus is mistaken for a woman, Billy is "all but feminine in purity of natural complexion" and is compared to a beautiful woman in a Hawthorne tale. Billy, like Séraphitus, exemplifies the externally beautiful, which Balzac believed to reflect moral perfection within:

> If some able physiologist had studied this being . . . he would undoubtedly had believed either in some phosphoric fluid of the nerves shining beneath the cuticle, or in the constant presence of an inward luminary, whose rays issued through the being of Seraphitus like a light through an alabaster vase. . . . Seraphitus appeared to grow in stature as he turned fully round and seemed about to spring upward. His hair, curled by a fairy's hand and waving to the breeze, increased the illusion produced by this aerial attitude; yet his bearing,

wholly without conscious effort, was the result far more of a moral phenomenon than of a corporeal habit."

Melville shares the belief that "the moral nature is seldom out of keeping with the physical make:"

> He was young; and despite his all but fully developed frame, in aspect looked even younger than he really was, owing to a lingering adolescent expression in the yet smooth face all but feminine in purity of natural complexion but where, thanks to his seagoing, the lily was quite suppressed and the rose has some ado visibly to flush through the tan . . . But the form of Billy Budd was heroic; . . . The bonfire in his heart made luminous the rose-tan in his cheek.

In Balzac's novel, the central character is the subject of the love of almost all around him, particularly Minna, Wilfrid, and the old servant, David. When Billy first appears, the narrator lets the reader know, through the captain of the *Rights of Man*, that a ruffian "really loves Billy—loves him or is the biggest hypocrite that ever I heard of" and we read later, that "Claggart could even have loved Billy but for fate and ban."

If the homosexual "camp" readings of Melville by contemporary critics like Robert K. Martin and James Creech are valid meters of Melville's sexual tendencies and the intuition of Brooks and Arvin is true, that Melville read *Séraphita* long before 1889, Melville's interest in *Séraphita* could prove to be more evasive than what can be traced from the evidence here. His modeling Budd's ambiguous sexuality on *Séraphita* could be more than philosophic romance; it could be a repeated personal identification at some psycho-social level of literary subterfuge. Balzac's novel may embody for Melville a very private reading that haunted him much of his life, one resonated with homoerotic feelings that according to these critics shaped many of his writing experiences.

This being considered, I nonetheless side with Parsons and view both Séraphita's and Billy Budd's sexuality as devised impersonally on the level of philosophy and in light of the esoteric tradition that informed both men rather than from repressed instincts or political statements about same-sex relationships. If my reading genuinely reflects Melville's convictions while finishing *Billy Budd*, an "absorbing interest" in this philosophy, his self indulging in instinct, even vicariously, would be unlikely. Besides, without any direct proof that Melville read *Séraphita* before 1889, we cannot connect empirically with this line of reasoning, which is supported primarily by earlier works, and we must be satisfied that the relationship between Séraphita and Billy Budd is primarily philosophical and aesthetic.

—John Haydock, "Melville's Séraphita: Billy Budd, Sailor" in *Melville Society Extracts* 104 (March 1996): pp. 12–13.

Works by
Herman Melville

"Fragments from a Writing Desk." 1839.

Typee. 1846.

Omoo. 1847.

Mardi. 1849.

Redburn. 1849.

White-Jacket. 1850.

Moby-Dick. 1851.

Pierre. 1852.

Israel Potter. 1855.

The Piazza Tales. 1856.

The Confidence-Man. 1857.

Battle-Pieces and Aspects of the War. 1866.

Clarel. 1876.

John Marr and Other Sailors. 1888.

Timoleon. 1891.

Billy Budd. 1924.

Collected Poems of Herman Melville. Ed. Howard P. Vincent. 1947.

Journal of a Visit to London and the Continent, 1849–1850. Ed. Eleanor Melville Metcalf. 1948.

The Letters of Herman Melville. Eds. Merrel R. David and William H. Gilman. 1960.

Weeds and Wildings Chiefly: With a Rose or Two. 1967.

Piazza Tales and Other Prose Pieces 1839–1860. Eds. Harrison Hayford, Alma MacDougall, and G. Thomas Tanselle. 1987.

Journals. Eds. Howard Horsford and Lynn Horth. 1989.

Correspondence. Ed. Lynn Horth. 1993.

Works about
Herman Melville

Allen, Gay Wilson. *Melville and His World*. New York: The Viking Press, 1971.

Arvin, Newton. *Herman Melville*. New York: William Sloane Associates, 1950.

Bartley, William. "'The Creature of His Own Tasteful Hands': Herman Melville's Benito Cereno and the 'Empire of Might.'" *Modern Philology* 93 (1996): 445–67.

Bergmann, Hans. "'Turkey on His Back': 'Bartleby' and New York Words." *Melville Society Extracts* 90 (1992): 16–19.

Berthoff, Warner. *The Example of Melville*. New York: W. W. Norton: 1972.

Berthold, Dennis. "Melville, Garibaldi, and the Medusa of Revolution." *American Literary History* 9 (1997): 425–59.

Bloom, Harold, ed. *Herman Melville's Billy Budd, "Benito Cereno," "Bartleby the Scrivener," and Other Tales*. New York: Chelsea House, 1987.

Borges, Jorge Luis. "Prologue to Herman Melville's 'Bartleby.'" *Latin American Literature and Art* 17 (1976): 24–25.

Bryant, John. *Melville and Repose: The Rhetoric of Humor in the American Renaissance*. New York: Oxford University Press, 1993.

Bryant, John, ed. *A Companion to Melville Studies*. Westport, Conn: Greenwood Press, 1986.

Budd, Louis J. and Cady, Edwin, eds. *On Melville: The Best From American Literature*. Durham, N.C.: Duke University Press, 1988.

Burkholder, Robert, ed. *Critical Essays on Melville's Benito Cereno*. Boston: G. K. Hall, 1996.

Busch, Frederick, ed. *Billy Budd and Other Stories*. New York: Penguin Books, 1986.

Clark, Michael. "Witches and Wall Street: Possession is Nine-Tenths of the Law." *Texas Studies in Literature and Language* 25 (1983): 55–76.

Donaldson, Scott. "The Dark Truth of *The Piazza Tales*." *PMLA* 85 (1970): 1082–86.

Dryden, Edgar A. "From the Piazza to the Enchanted Isles: Melville's Textual Rovings." In Jay and Miller's *After Strange Texts: The Role of*

Theory in the Study of Literature. Montgomery, Ala.: University of Alabama Press, 1985.

Ferguson, Robert A. "Untold Stories in the Law." In Brooks and Gewirtz's *Law's Stories: Narrative and Rhetoric in the Law.* New Haven: Yale University Press, 1996.

Franklin, H. Bruce. "Apparent Symbol of Despotic Command: Melville's Benito Cereno." *New England Quarterly* 34 (1961): 23–34.

Garner, Stanton. *The Civil War World of Herman Melville.* Lawrence, Kan.: University Press of Kansas, 1993.

Guttmann, Allen. "The Enduring Innocence of Captain Amasa Delano." *Boston University Studies in English* 5 (1961): 35–45.

Hans, James S. "Emptiness and Plenitude in 'Bartleby the Scrivener' and *The Crying of Lot 49.*" *Essays in Literature* 22 (1995): 285–99.

Hattenhauer, Darryl. "Ambiguities of Time in Melville's 'The Encantadas.'" *American Transcendental Quarterly* 56 (1985): 5–17.

Haydock, John. "Melville's Séraphita: Billy Budd, Sailor," *Melville Society Extracts* (1996): 2–13.

Hillway, Tyrus. *Herman Melville.* New York: Twayne, 1963.

Howard, Leon. *Herman Melville: A Biography.* Berkeley: University of California Press, 1967.

Jaffe, David. *"Bartleby the Scrivener" and "Bleak House": Melville's Debt to Dickens.* Arlington, Va.: Mardi Press, 1981.

Johnson, Barbara. "Melville's Fist: the Execution of Billy Budd." *Studies in Romanticism* 18 (1979): 567–99.

Jones, Gavin. "Dusky Comments of Silence: Language, Race, and Herman Melville's 'Benito Cereno.'" *Studies in Short Fiction* 32 (1995): 39–50.

Karcher, Carolyn. "The Riddle of the Sphinx, Melville's Benito Cereno and the Amistad Case." In *Burkholder's Critical Essays on Melville's Benito Cereno.* Boston: G. K. Hall, 1996.

Leyda, Jay. *The Melville Log: A Documentary Life of Herman Melville, 1819–1891,* 2 vols. New York: Harcourt, Brace, 1951.

Mansfield, Luther S. "Glimpses of Herman Melville's Life in Pittsfield." *American Literature* 9 (1937): 26–48.

Marx, Leo. "Melville's Parable of the Walls." *Sewanee Review* 61 (1953): 602–27.

Matthiessen, F. O. *American Renaissance.* New York: Oxford University Press, 1941.

Mayoux, Jean-Jacques. *Melville.* Translated by John Ashbery. New York: Grove Press, 1960.

McCall, Dan. *The Silence of Bartleby.* Ithaca: Cornell University Press, 1989.

Milder, Robert, ed. *Critical Essays on Melville's Billy Budd, Sailor.* Boston: G. K. Hall, 1989.

Mitchell, Thomas R. "Dead Letters and Dead Men: Narrative Purpose in 'Bartleby, the Scrivener.'" *Studies in Short Fiction* 27 (1990): 329–38.

Mumford, Lewis. *Herman Melville: A Study of His Life and Vision.* New York: Harcourt, Brace, and Co., 1929. (Reissued in a revised edition, London: Secker & Warburg, 1963.)

Newbery, I. "'The Encantadas': Melville's Inferno." *American Literature* 38 (1966): 49–68.

Nnolim, Charles E. *Melville's "Benito Cereno": A Study in Meaning of Name Symbolism.* New York: New Voices Publishing, 1974.

Pahl, Dennis. "The Gaze of History in 'Benito Cereno.'" *Studies in Short Fiction* 32 (1995): 171–83.

Phillips, Kathy J. "Billy Budd as Anti-Homophobic Text." *College English* 56 (1994): 896–910.

Post-Lauria, Shelia. "Canonical Text and Context: The Example of Herman Melville's Bartleby the Scrivener: A Story of Wall Street." *College Literature* 20 (1993): 196–205.

Ra'ad, Basem L. "'The Encantadas' and 'The Isle of the Cross': Melvillean Dubieties, 1853–54." *American Literature* 63 (1991): 316–23.

Radloff, Bernhard. *Will and Representation: The Philosophical Foundations of Melville's Theatrum Mundi.* New York: Lang, 1996.

Robertson-Lorant, Laurie. *Melville: A Biography.* New York: Clarkson Potter, 1996.

Rogin, Michael. *Subversive Genealogy: The Politics and Art of Herman Melville.* New York: Knopf, 1983.

Schaub, Diana J. "Master and Man in Melville's 'Benito Cereno.'" In Knippenberg and Lawler's *Poets, Princes, and Private Citizens: Literary Alternatives to Postmodern Politics.* Lanham, Md.: Rowman & Littlefield, 1996.

Sealts, Merton M., Jr. *The Early Lives of Melville: Nineteenth-Century Biographical Sketches and Their Authors.* Madison: University of Wisconsin Press, 1974.

Shattuck, Roger. "Guilt, Justice, and Empathy in Melville and Camus." *Partisan Review* 63 (1996): 430–49.

Simpson, Eleanor M. "Melville and the Negro: From *Typee* to 'Benito Cereno.'" In *On Melville: The Best From American Literature*, Louis J. Budd and Edwin Cady, eds. Durham, N.C.: Duke University Press, 1988.

Sundquist, Eric J. "'Benito Cereno' and New World Slavery." In Sacvan Bercovitch's *Reconstructing American Literary History*. Cambridge: Harvard University Press, 1986.

———. "Suspense and Tautology in "Benito Cereno." *Glyph: Johns Hopkins Textual Studies* 8 (1981): 103–126.

Weiner, Susan. "'Benito Cereno' and the Failure of Law." *Arizona Quarterly* 47 (1991): 1–28.

———. *Law in Art: Melville's Major Fiction and Nineteenth-Century American Law*. New York: Peter Lang Publishing, 1992.

Wenke, John. *Melville's Muse: Literary Creation and the Forms of Philosophical Fiction*. Kent, Ohio: Kent State University Press, 1995.

Winters, Yvor. *In Defense of Reason*. Denver: Allan Swallow, 1947.

Yarina, Margaret. "The Dualistic Vision of Herman Melville's 'The Encantadas.'" *Journal of Narrative Technique* 3 (1973): 141–48.

Index of
Themes and Ideas